A Transformative Future with AI

Michael Torrence PhD

A Transformative Future with AI

We all have a perspective that could be incorporated into the discussion on the importance of institutions and educators understanding the possibilities and limitations of AI tools like ChatGPT. We should posit that an emphasis on the necessity of comprehensive education and training for educators, focusing on AI literacy and competency is in short order. Pundits, society at large, and policymakers may express concerns regarding the potential for AI to distribute inaccurate or biased information, reinforcing the need for a critical thinking component in AI integration. However, as any technological tool, AI will take the spaces we code for its advancement.

An iterative development and evaluation in using AI tools for educational purposes is important. The implementation of any such technology must be continuously monitored, evaluated, and improved to maximize its social benefit and minimize potential risks. We must advance policy around AI. I would stress the importance of robust policy formation around AI usage in education, underscoring the need for collaboration between educators, technologists, workforce, policy makers, and students to ensure a responsible and beneficial implementation of AI across educational and industry settings.

As we continue to lament the future of work, training, learning, and innovation, we can envision a shift towards a more adaptive, personalized, and continuous learning system, facilitated by AI and digital technologies. This evolution will not exclude human beings but create a broader economy surrounding integrative skills. Healthcare, advanced manufacturing, logistics and supply chain, sales, and the spirits industry serve as exemplars in the utilization of forward moving tech.

As the future of work changes, driven by AI and automation, there will be an increasing demand for both technical skills and durable skills. Therefore, continuous learning and re-skilling will become essential, and the role of education and training will need to evolve accordingly. I wonder what linemen and HVAC persons will gain from integration of these tools and platforms.

Moreover, workforce and educational organizations will link the rise of micro-credentials and alternative credentials significance as part of this future landscape. These allow individuals to continually update their skills and knowledge in a fast-changing job market. They may become the norm, as people seek to learn throughout their careers rather than just at the start. Learning is indeed on a continuum and technology has already changed how we learn, making education more interactive, collaborative, and immersive. Virtual reality, augmented reality, and AI might transform classrooms, providing experiences that are more engaging and tailored to individual learners' needs. Conversely, I'll reiterate the importance of human centered design as necessary.

The integration of AI and other advanced technologies into education and the workplace will drive new ways of thinking and problem-solving. The intersection of these technologies with diverse fields could lead to unprecedented innovation, creating new industries and job categories that we can't even envision today. Here is a list of potential policies a state or national group may review, undertake, or develop to evolve the landscape of work, learning, and AI:

1. Education Policies: Policies should be updated to reflect a focus on lifelong learning, promoting both technical and durable skills. This could involve incorporating more flexible and personalized learning paths, like micro-credentials and alternative credentials, into mainstream education.
2. AI Ethics and Transparency: Policies should be developed to ensure the ethical use of AI in education and the workplace. This could include guidelines for data privacy, algorithmic fairness, and transparency, so users understand how AI tools are affecting their learning or work.
3. Digital Access and Literacy: Policies should be in place to ensure digital equity – all students, regardless of their socioeconomic background, should have access to digital tools and internet connectivity. Additionally, there should be a strong focus on building digital literacy from a young age.
4. Teacher Training and Support: Policies should provide resources and training for teachers to effectively integrate AI and other technologies into their teaching.
5. Recognition of Alternative Credentials: There should be policies that ensure broader recognition of micro-credentials and other alternative credentials, so that they are valued by higher education institutions and employers.
6. Workforce Development and Re-skilling: Policies could be designed to encourage businesses to invest in continuous training and development for their employees, preparing them for the evolving demands of the job market.
7. Cross-Sector Collaboration: Policies should foster collaboration between educational institutions, businesses, and government to address the changing needs of the future workforce and align educational outcomes with labor market needs.
8. Regulation of AI and Emerging Technologies: Policies are needed to regulate the use of AI and other emerging technologies, including provisions for safety, accountability, and misuse prevention.

In conclusion, the way forward is currently occurring for Tennesseans who work, train, and learn. Simply put, we all will be heavily influenced by the policies and decisions we make today. Our future remains brightest when we commingle the importance of designing inclusive, forward-thinking policies to ensure that everyone can benefit from these changes, and no one is left behind.

Othering Toward Community Development

What happens if we emphasized the importance of making education and job training accessible and effective for individuals from various marginalized or underrepresented groups? Let us think of including those who have been involved with the justice system, those who have aged out of foster care, veterans, and incumbent workers. Our collective "doing so" would highlight the necessity for tailored educational and training programs to meet the unique needs of these individuals. Moreover, this would include socio-emotional support, mentorship, and targeted skill development.

We have additional, not alternative, policy considerations that might include deepening the creation of our interactive matrices for individuals who are justice-involved. We have metrics that show 95% of all who are justice -involved, ultimately returning home. Justice-involved individuals, and our community economies, would certainly strengthen if policies could encourage the development of vocational training and educational programs within and outside of correctional facilities. Additionally, anti-discrimination policies could be established to ensure these individuals have fair opportunities in the workforce post-incarceration. There are far too many opportunities available to Tennessean's who want to work. Let's continue to ramp up training options as early as possible and put people to work.

Aging out of foster care is an inevitable outcome for some youth. Support exists for giving programs that could categorically assist these young adults transition into adulthood include educational scholarships, mentorship programs, and job training initiatives. Policies may also address the need for stable housing and mental health support. Utilizing linked public services for housing, food, and job training will alter the landscape for the better. We have a need to close more gaps and plug more holes created by advances in teaching and learning for all disparate groups.

Policies for Veterans may ensure that skills acquired during military service are recognized and transferrable in the civilian workforce. We have and will continue doing our best to right-size this transition. We still may find ourselves in situations where Veterans key skills exceed our goals, competencies, and training objectives, but not all can translate for probability. Our support for continued education and reintegration programs could certainly continue to be enhanced.

Further, the incumbent workers whose lifelong learning pedigree should merit credentials, seeks clarity. The policies established may need continued review and alterations for incumbent workers to continually upgrade their skills and adapt to changing job requirements. Adjustments for this group also includes programs for digital literacy and upskilling to meet the needs of a changing economy. We must continue to highlight the needed technical skills for CDL's, HVAC, and Automation, Fabrication, and Robotics and we must usher in the aggressive conversation supporting surrounding Data Science, Cyber Security Architect, Cloud Manager, and a host of others. These job skills are in demand and meet rural Tennessean's right where they are, learning/training from localized Community and Technical Colleges.

Policies implications underscore the importance of addressing systemic barriers and providing comprehensive support, from education to job placement, to these previously mentioned populations. Advocacy for evolutionary reform could lead to a more broadly inclusive workforce.

If we consider the promise of emerging technologies in training/learning, we find ourselves at the intersection of access, engagement, and innovation. Mobile tools, augmented reality, and artificial intelligence, all have the power to democratize education, and indeed, the workforce. Thus, this may justly widen the threshold for economic and community development and engagement.

We must ensure that our policies nurture this potential. Let's envision digital literacy not as a privilege, but as a right, pushing for strong digital infrastructure across all communities. This is a necessary step towards digital equity.

The elephant in the room is most certainly, on the matter of privacy and data security, that we must thread a delicate balance. The key is to harness the power of data for personalized learning/training while upholding the highest standards of privacy. This is not a trade-off, but a commitment we must make to our learners and trainees. In the same vein, let's view AI not as a replacement for human interaction, but as a tool to enrich it. Artificial intelligence can offer a tailored learning/training pathway for everyone, but we cannot forget the value of mentorship, collaboration, and social learning.

The integration of AR and AI into our curriculum should be done thoughtfully. It's not about technology for technology's sake, but about how these tools can truly enhance the learning process. How can AR provide richer, more engaging vocational training? How can AI help us understand and address the learning gaps? How can AI help us close skill gaps?

The path forward is collaboration. It involves educators, technologists, policymakers, and learners themselves. By working together, we can truly harness the power of these technologies to create an equitable, engaging, and effective learning/training environment. Wherever we go, that's where we will be. Please see a few ideas for consideration. What happens next?

Let's not forget the crucial role of our educators/faculty in this process. They are not merely bystanders, but key players. We need to equip them with the necessary skills and knowledge, not only so they can use these technologies but also so they can critically evaluate their use. The development of educators/faculty will be a great determinant to our immediate, interim, and long-term future.

Short-Term (1-2 years): We should expect increased awareness and discussions around digital literacy and the potential of AR and AI in education and workforce. What do we

foresee as the initial steps being taken to improve digital infrastructure and reduce the digital skills divide?
Along with an uptick in collaborations between educational institutions and tech companies, we will see broadening the scope of a 3P (Public Private Partnership). A move away from pilot programs using AI and AR in various learning contexts and a move towards the integration of our disparate platforms to a Universally Integrated System (UIS).

Medium-Term (3-5 years): We may anticipate broader integration of AR and AI in both K-12 and higher education settings, alongside a more widespread adoption of mobile learning tools. The creation of new policies supporting digital learning and protecting student data is inevitable, along with substantial improvements in personalized, AI-driven learning experiences. The first concrete outcomes from earlier initiatives to reduce the digital divide might begin to manifest, including increased digital literacy rates and improved access to digital resources among disadvantaged populations.

Long-Term (5-10 years): Might we also predict a complete transformation of the learning landscape, with AR, AI, quantum computing and mobile learning becoming the norm rather than the exception. We can expect robust data privacy protections being developed and out in place. This will balance the needs for personalized learning and privacy. The future also aligns with a more equitable learning environment, with digital tools helping to level the playing field for learners of different backgrounds (my optimism speaking). Lastly, we can also expect substantial improvements in workforce readiness because of these educational transformations, with a workforce that is better prepared for the demands of an increasingly digital and automated economy.

MARYLOU APPLE
SCIENCE - TECHNOLOGY - ALLIED HEALTH
MOTLOW STATE

Motlow State Community College: The State of-Training and Learning

Motlow State Community College continues its trajectory as a present and forward leaning institution. The college commits to exhibit proactive approaches as we prepare for today's learner, earner, and owner. The learner is our student. The earner is our employed graduate, and the owner is the business/industry/entrepreneurial partner utilizing our workforce programs to advance their brand/meet their employment needs. Our passion for student success has continued to transition additional graduates early through our dual enrollment program. This past May 8th, Motlow State Community College graduated 87 dual enrollment students with associate degrees prior to these students receiving their high school diplomas. We are certainly proud of the students, our faculty, and our local high school partnerships that make this possible.

Additionally, our partners exercise ongoing engagement as we build our programs of study in consultation with stakeholders as disparate as students and broad industry needs. We can ensure that needs are being met through affordable education that emphasizes the importance of accessing learning and the role of education. Currently, we are over 18 months into an imitative called the Metaversity that will provide verifiable portable credentials to our students. This scalable launch provides students with micro credentials they can take anywhere in the palms of their hands. As we see the ongoing decentralization of personally identifiable information (PII), this platform services become more important. We are advocating for continuity within our communities where learning and the role of durable skills positively impact the creation of a decent society. We know that there are imperfections to the delivery modalities we have employed, but we have not only acknowledged this, but we have also inserted more hands-on learning, more experiential learning, and more necessary disruption to the status quo in our field. Our faculty have invested time in re-learning and evolving our stronger blended learning, open education resource (OER), and meta skilled instructional practices. Motlow State Community College faculty are leaders locally and regionally with the arsenal of instructional modalities they have at their fingertips.

Motlow State constantly evaluates our digital strategies to grapple with the potential impact we will have on students and employer partners. We know that online learning holds a great breadth of opportunity due to its flexibility and alignment with modern workforce demands. We link the synchronous and the asynchronous learning experiences while focusing on engaging, high-quality content. Conversely, a universal instructional platform does not exist, yet so we will continue to have an open campus to welcome all learners who continue to advantage themselves through face to face on ground classroom instruction. One of our goals is to provide learning environments that mirror the interactive and collaborative nature of seamless learning environments. At Motlow State, learn anything, learn anywhere, learn anytime, and learn with everyone.

We see the future of education as an exciting blend of traditional pedagogical, andragogical, methods and cutting-edge technology. The integration of technology will continue to be an indispensable part of learning and training. Motlow State Community College will continuously explore ways to harness the potential of technology and leverage the capabilities of human centered design for our students' benefit.

The rise of artificial intelligence (AI) and machine learning will revolutionize the way we teach, learn, train, and innovate. We are actively exploring how these technologies can enhance personalized learning, improve student engagement, and provide real time effective feedback. In the realm of aviation, we are leveraging advanced simulators to provide practical, hands-on experience to pilots and trainees. This model of experiential learning continues our vision to expand across into other disciplines as well. Although we have yet to invest in quantum computing and big data networks, we recognize the impact and reshaping of industries, and education is not exempt. We will continue to seek methods to integrate emerging content into our curriculum so that we can provide our students valuable skills in data analysis and problem solving.

Universally integrated systems represent a new frontier in collaboration and productivity. We see the immense potential in these systems to facilitate seamless communication, improve regional development, and enhance the overall learning/training experience. Overall, this approach signifies a move towards an even more student-centered model that is less transactional and more transformative. This values the individual learner's needs, interests, and career goals. Moreover, this provides a direct stairwell from education to employment. This not only enhances the value of education for students, but also contributes to a more skilled and competent workforce. Ultimately, our goal is to ensure our students are not just consumers of technology, but also creators and critical evaluators. By integrating mapped skill development alongside technology into our curriculum, the Motlow State Community College student will leave both hands on prepared and a more attractive employee candidate for the digital present of today's workforce.

Necessary Disruptions: Advancing Education Through Universally Integrated Systems, Quantum Computing, and Dual Enrollment

In an ever-evolving global landscape, it becomes increasingly crucial to leverage the power of quantum data, particularly in government agencies, business and industry, and higher education. Our Connected States have a rich blend of these sectors, and are all ideally positioned to benefit from a universal integrated system (UIS) for quantum data linked to dual enrollment and other systems.

Quantum computing, characterized by its capacity for massive data processing and sophisticated algorithms, could offer a transformative leap in how we handle data. For government agencies, this technology could enhance operations and public services. It could optimize resource allocation, improve traffic management, enhance cybersecurity, and even predict social trends or environmental changes. Imagine having the clearest trend data based on the last several years of Bonnaroo (Coffee County), CMA FEST (Davidson County), the Jack Daniel BBQ (Moore County), just to name a few, where metros and small-town rural areas could optimize economic impact with less waste?

In business and industry, the adoption of quantum data could revolutionize practices. Companies could use this technology for supply chain optimization, risk assessment, and financial modeling, among other applications. Industries such as healthcare could see remarkable improvements in drug discovery, patient recovery, patient data management, and disease modeling. Could we see the cure to disease and viruses that we now call incurable during this lifetime? Might we learn what conditions optimize accelerated recovery and mitigate risks on a patient-by-patient basis?

Higher education, as both a consumer and producer of quantum technology, stands to benefit immensely. Community and Technical Colleges, Public and Private Universities can integrate quantum computing into their applied research endeavors, driving breakthroughs in fields as varied as logistics, health sciences, data science, cloud architecture, physics, chemistry, computer science, and economics. Moreover, aligning human design to shore up the success of each individual taking courses, training, and employed by the organization. Protection and privacy are paramount. At the same time, higher education can play a critical role in preparing the next generation of quantum scientists and engineers. We have an opportunity to intertwine curricular and industry points of emphasis simultaneously. Groundbreaking developments have taken place as early as preschool that introduce basic concepts of spatial computing - VR and AR. Our youth should not only be consumers of tomorrow, but builders of the future as well. Let's expand and continue to use "play" as a methodology children and incumbent workers utilize for their development.

Creating a universal integrated system for quantum data access, however, will require a concerted and collaborative effort across all sectors. Public-private partnerships could provide the funding and expertise necessary to develop this infrastructure. Simultaneously, legislative support for data privacy and security regulations would ensure the ethical and safe use of quantum data. Moreover, we need experts, visionaries, industry, and government around one table to make this viable. Segmented situated pontificating will land us where we are, no closer to a final design or applicable minimum viable product. An accelerated approach is called for to pop out the creases of the higher education archaic grooves. We need metamorphosis!

The goal of strengthening education in modern ways can begin with clarifying the economic implications of dual enrollment. Commitment without currency is not only fraudulent, but also counterfeit. Leveraging blended learning and open education resources (OER), positions micro credentials as ongoing for the lifelong learning necessary in the job market.

Dual enrollment programs, which allow high school students to earn college credits, offer promising avenues for advancing educational attainment. However, these programs are not without economic implications, particularly regarding flat cost, access, labor market preparation, and the support of socioeconomically disadvantaged students. Further, support for socioeconomically disadvantaged students could come in the form of improved counseling services, targeted outreach, and wraparound supports like tutoring and transportation. Inclusive dual enrollment policies, like universally allowing all high school students to participate regardless of GPA, would increase graduates and employable skilled workers.

The cost of dual enrollment programs is a multifaceted opportunity. While students may ostensibly seem to save money by reducing the time and cost of college, the burden of their costs often falls unevenly on various parties. Often, school districts, colleges, students, or a combination of these bear the expense. Reducing or eliminating these costs for students—particularly those from low-income backgrounds—is critical to making these programs genuinely accessible. Access to dual enrollment programs is closely linked to cost, but there are other issues at play. Geographic, academic, and bureaucratic barriers can restrict student access. Rural students, for example, often have fewer dual enrollment opportunities due to the distance from postsecondary institutions. Policymakers must think creatively about mitigating these challenges, possibly through online education, transportation solutions, or partnerships with colleges to offer more courses in high schools.

The goal of dual enrollment programs is not only to provide college credit but also to prepare students for the labor market. Students who participate in these programs are more likely to graduate high school, attend college, and earn a degree—all of which increase employment prospects and potential earnings. The work-readiness and practical skills offered through dual enrollment programs, particularly those with a career and technical education (CTE) focus, are a significant boon to students entering the workforce directly from high school.

For socioeconomically disadvantaged students, the benefits of dual enrollment can be especially significant. However, these students often face the largest barriers to participation. Free or reduced-cost dual enrollment programs can provide these students with a lifeline to higher education and a pathway out of poverty. However, cost is only one barrier; we also need to address issues like college readiness, academic support, and access to information about these programs.

Ultimately, the success of dual enrollment programs hinges on their economic feasibility for all students, not just those with ample resources. Policymakers must carefully consider the costs of these programs and who bears them, work to expand access beyond traditional barriers, and ensure that these programs effectively prepare students for the workforce. With thoughtful policy and practice, dual enrollment programs have the potential to be a vital tool for social mobility and economic progression. Dual enrollment programs, like those incorporating STEAMB(e), could serve as an excellent conduit for quantum education at the high school level. Providing early access to quantum concepts can create a pipeline of quantum-literate students poised to fill the future needs of the workforce.

Moreover, collaboration with higher education institutions can help align dual enrollment programs with the requirements of quantum-related fields of study. This way, students could gain an early start on the path to quantum careers while contributing to the local talent pool. The promise of quantum data is immense, but so too are the challenges in developing the infrastructure and talent necessary to fully exploit this promise. By committing to a universal integrated system that democratizes access to quantum data, Tennessee could position itself as a leader in the quantum revolution, fostering economic growth, social advancement, and educational opportunities in the process.

Ultimately, the even more broad success of dual enrollment programs hinges on their economic feasibility for all students, not just those with ample resources. Policymakers must carefully consider the costs of these programs and who bears them, work to expand access beyond traditional barriers, and ensure that these programs effectively prepare students for the workforce. With thoughtful policy and practice, dual enrollment programs have the potential to be a vital tool for social mobility and economic equality.

In summary, universally integrated systems, quantum computing, and dual enrollment covers an impressive array of disciplines that will shape the future of our economy and society. By incorporating these fields/approaches into dual enrollment programs and linking to OER, we can better prepare students for a wide range of careers and foster a workforce capable of meeting the challenges of the 21st century. In the long run, this will not only strengthen our economy but also ensure that we are ready to innovate and adapt to whatever the future may bring.

MOTLOW STATE
COMMUNITY COLLEGE
MOTLOW STATE
COMMUNITY COLLEGE

Navigating the Interplay of AI, Privacy, Blockchain, and Policy/Governance: Envisioning the Future of Networks

The interplay between artificial intelligence (AI), privacy, blockchain, and policy/governance is shaping the future of networks. The aim of these string of words is to provide insights into this intricate landscape and shed light on the implications it holds for society. In this essay, we will explore the potential of AI, the criticality of privacy, the transformative power of blockchain, and the necessity of robust policy/governance frameworks.

AI can be a catalyst for transformation, isn't it already? Artificial intelligence has emerged as a transformative force across industries, revolutionizing the way we live and work. AI-driven systems possess the ability to process vast amounts of data, derive meaningful insights, and make informed decisions. We have already, and literally for decades, been exposed to AI developments. Logistics, healthcare, automation, electric vehicles are but a few co-locations where AI intersects with our current day-to-day. However, this immense potential comes with ethical considerations. Who owns the data? Can you relinquish your right to your data? Is your data for use or purchase? I know this gets at decentralized autonomous organizations (DOA) too, but that is not for this discussion. Privacy concerns arise as personal data becomes fuel for AI algorithms. Striking the right balance between leveraging AI's power and safeguarding privacy is essential for a sustainable future.

The imperative of privacy protection will only continue to be wrestled with in a space that is not democratized. This "network" must be all inclusive. The ubiquity of networks and the pervasive nature of AI raise concerns about privacy infringement. At what point does your privacy become open to review and scrutiny? Who owns your SSN? Will we need new assigned "digits"? Are we digitizing and linking all private information into public-private systems? As individuals interact with interconnected devices, their personal information is collected, analyzed, and utilized. Preserving privacy in this digital age necessitates comprehensive data protection regulations and technological safeguards. It is imperative that individuals maintain control over their data, with transparency and informed consent as foundational principles. By striking a delicate equilibrium between AI-driven innovation and privacy protection, we can harness the potential of networks for the betterment of society. This is a space where Trust networks will be increasingly, not only important, but permeably permanent. The network has to have the ability to evolve with the person and visa versa.

Blockchain is a place for us to build trust and security. In the face of increasing digitization, blockchain technology presents a decentralized solution to enhance trust, security, and transparency within networks. Through its immutable and distributed ledger, blockchain offers an innovative approach to data management, ensuring the integrity and reliability of transactions. It has the potential to revolutionize sectors such as finance, supply chain management, and healthcare, fostering efficiency and accountability. However, the adoption of blockchain requires careful consideration of scalability, interoperability, and regulatory frameworks to fully unlock its transformative potential. Motlow State Community College has launched its digital skills wallet, Metaversity. The verifiable blockchain enabled digital wallet was built in 5 months in partnership with the Learning Economy Foundation and DXtera. A $500K grant from the Tennessee Higher Education Commission (THEC) funded the development of Phase I. Motlow State has deployed Metaversity to 100 students in our Mechatronics and Robotics programs. We have a portable solution for our students to show their skills to anyone, anywhere, anytime, and on demand. Most recently, we provided the National Governors Association, Jobs For the Future, and Vantage Consulting with a snapshot of our work from the student perspective. We believe that the meaning and lessons taken from our student representatives provided all in earshot a clearer picture of our use case. Our goal is to scale this model across our institution and continue to support our students and employers. We are utilizing our approaches, parts of our next wave would be to utilize our meta-tools to hire employees.

Navigating the policy/governance in the future will be a continuous process. As networks evolve and intertwine with AI, privacy, and blockchain, policy and governance frameworks must adapt accordingly. Are we prepared for the adaptations necessary? Do we have enough of a knowledge base to make informed decisions? Obviously, governments and regulatory bodies will play a crucial role in establishing guidelines that encourage innovation, ensure network security, and protect individual rights. The question raised is how I touch with what is emergent are they in order to regulate its nuances? Collaborative efforts are needed to address the challenges posed by emerging technologies, such as AI bias, data breaches, and algorithmic transparency. Policymakers must strike a balance between pausing to paralysis and fostering innovation while safeguarding societal interests. The continuity between establishing ethical standards and legal frameworks to govern the deployment of network technologies is paramount.

The social implications of AI are stretched. The interplay of AI, privacy, blockchain, and policy/governance has far-reaching implications for society. On one hand, AI-driven networks hold immense potential for economic growth, improved healthcare, personalized education, and enhanced decision-making processes. On the other hand, concerns over privacy breaches, algorithmic bias, and the digital divide loom large. As we shape the future of networks, we must ensure that technology serves as an equalizer, bridging societal gaps and empowering individuals. This is a large gap to fill. Does it not expand constantly? Closing this hole requires "wrap-around" policies, ethical practices, and comprehensive educational initiatives to prepare individuals for the networked world of today and tomorrow.

As we navigate the complex relationship between AI, privacy, blockchain, and policy/governance, it's crucial to acknowledge their profound impact on the future of networks and society as a whole. Striking a harmonious balance becomes essential, combining innovation and progress with ethical considerations and protection of individual rights. Our effectiveness relies on moving together as a unified force. This moment is transformative, demanding intertwined collective approaches. To achieve this, we must embrace responsible AI development, prioritize privacy safeguards, harness the transformative potential of blockchain, and establish robust policies. Additionally, international collaboration in policy making can streamline safeguards, enabling nations to learn and grow together. The work has already begun, and we must continue together.

The Transformative Rise of OER: Empowering Students and Enhancing Learning

Open Educational Resources (OER) have continued to gain momentum in academia, specifically, as an economic betterment. Motlow State Community College, embracing the pedagogical and economic advantages of OER, has seen a surge in enrollments in OER courses, especially since the fall of 2020. Although our commitment to OER began years prior, the full throttle had yet to be pushed. We must note that the critical role of technology in promoting and facilitating the integration of OER should be explored. OER has thrived on digital platforms, allowing for real-time updates, an array of multimedia elements, and easy sharing. The growing connectivity has enabled students to access resources from anywhere, anytime. Moreover, educational institutions have adopted/co-managed Learning Management Systems (LMS) that can effectively integrate OER, making it a seamless component of the curriculum. Through collaboration and unwavering commitment, the college has made remarkable strides in integrating OER into its curriculum.

Between fall 2020 and fall 2022, there has been a commendable growth in OER course enrollments at Motlow. The percentage of students enrolled in at least one OER course has risen from 59% to 64%. More impressively, the enrollment in two or more OER courses climbed from 23% to 30% during the same period. These trends are mirrored in Dual Enrollment (DE) students, where 55% of all DE course enrollment in fall 2022 were in OER courses, up from 44% in fall 2020. These are important signals and inflection points as higher education sees growth in this demographic area.

The number of OER sections offered experienced a substantial growth of 19.7% between fall 2020 and fall 2021, and a remarkable 53.8% increase from fall 2021 to fall 2022. This demonstrates the college's commitment to making education more accessible and affordable. This also reflects the obvious desire from the student to leverage access to flexible resources.

A shining example of OER's impact/growth is in the BIOL 1010 course. Between fall 2020 and fall 2022, the percentage of students taking BIOL 1010 as an OER course escalated dramatically, culminating in all sections of BIOL 1010 being offered as OER courses in fall 2022. The success rates in the course increased by over 10% between fall 2021 and fall 2022, and by 15% when comparing regular to OER sections.

Another area where OER has proven to be significantly beneficial is History. According to Dr. Melody Edmonds, former Assistant Vice President for Academic Affairs at Motlow and current President at Tennessee College of Applied Technology at McMinnville, the transition to fully OER in all History classes in fall 2020 resulted in a 4% increase in student success rates among Pell-eligible students. Success in this space does not occur without faculty and their leadership. During this adaptation, our team of faculty was continually adjusting to our students' needs. The faculty contributions and universal design play a large role in our academic nimbleness.

The growth of OER at Motlow is the result of diligent work by the faculty. They have recorded lectures and modified open-source materials to meet the unique needs of Motlow students. Feedback from students has been pivotal in this process, guiding efforts to enhance student achievement. OER supports the Universal Design of Learning by offering accessible and relevant content that caters to the diverse needs of students. Our student voices have agency here and with it, we will continue to see them take great strides. Alongside the student, we are better able to construct not only curricular reshaped, but services that better support or prepare them for their next steps. Conversely, there are potential challenges. While OER is significantly advantageous, deconstructionists may have concerns regarding the quality of content, and the need for continual updates to maintain relevancy should be addressed. Currently, our faculty build, design, and maintain our courses. Therefore, it is with a high level of confidence we support expansion and the further development of our Academic Resource Center, (ARC), which is the training and learning academy space for faculty in conjunction with our Motlow Libraries. Moreover, not all educators are familiar or comfortable with OER, and may require professional development and support to effectively integrate them into their teaching. We believe our Observe Orient Decide Act (OODA) loop is sound.

We can also delve into the broader impact of OER on education. While Motlow State Community College serves as a case study, the comparative literature has not been explored at this time from state to state. The democratization of knowledge through OER can have profound implications in narrowing education disparities, and fostering a culture of lifelong learning. Portable learning is currently in our grasp, at our fingertip's reach, and/or by tracking our eyes. As more employers expect results and a ready-made workforce, preparation is central to successful hires. The role of OER in supporting the development of critical thinking and adaptability among students should be noted. With OER, students are not just passive recipients but active contributors to the content. They too can identify and report adjustments in real time to content or advancements in the field. This engagement fosters a culture of inquiry and self-directed learning.

Our collaborations within the state have also yielded great points of entry for the learner. OER materials developed are housed in the TN Open Education Hub, making these resources accessible not only to the local community but also to a global audience. This initiative reflects Motlow's role in the larger educational ecosystem. Additionally, it furthers a disruption to education desserts and provides a key point of access.

The future prospects of OER align with the advancements in artificial intelligence and virtual reality. We believe the possibilities for enhancing OER are boundless. The subject-matter areas are simply mind-boggling for the spirits, culinary, hospitality and tourism industries are but one array of exemplars. Additionally, CTE and STEM areas will find broader success and higher engagement. The development of adaptive learning systems that tailor content to individual needs, or immersive learning experiences through virtual reality, can take OER to new heights. This is an opportunity for Motlow State Community College and other institutions to stay at the forefront of education by continuously innovating and embracing emerging technologies.

The rise of OER at Motlow State Community College is a testament to the transformative potential of open education. Our deliberate and ecosystem building approaches are now flourishing. Our students lean into learning in the same fashion that we all lean into anything, when those around you support your failure, fatigue, and fanaticism. We want to see everyone succeed. Our faculty are committed to the arts of teaching, learning, and innovation. Through faculty engagement, student feedback, and institutional support, OER is proving to be an empowering tool for learners, significantly reducing costs, and enhancing educational outcomes.

innovate
create
build
prove
test
certify

Metaversity

Classified as a small rural community college best known for its transfer programs, RN degree, and mechatronics, one may not think about Motlow College being on the cutting edge of the very latest technology known as metaversity.

However, in less than one year, Motlow College and partners, the Learning Economy Foundation (LEF) and the DXtera Institute, created a digital wallet that students can use to record all credentials, grades, skills, and other information they might choose to include on an application on their phones, making this information immediately accessible to them and those with whom they choose to share.

The project was the vision of Motlow College President Dr. Michael Torrence who saw the value of a digital wallet phone application that can be used to maintain a permanent cumulative record of educational and work-related credentials in one place.

According to Dr. Torrence, "Our goal was to create a portable platform that allowed our communities the ability to immediately display the credentials and skills they learned. Our Metaversity application simply identifies a central method of displaying authentic verifiable blockchain credentials. We will advance further versions to have even more robust use. This will help our students and our employers."

After contacting the Tennessee Higher Education Commission (THEC) for support and approval to proceed, a workgroup of Motlow staff and faculty and industry partners began the work of bringing Dr. Torrence's idea from conception to implementation. Their progress was shared recently with representatives of the National Governors Association (NGA), and Jobs for the Future (JFF),) organizations which traditionally support the scaling of revolutionary ideas in education and workforce development. Other stakeholders in attendance were members of THEC and a representative from Vantage Point Consulting, Motlow State faculty, staff and student representatives.

In his introduction of the work, Dr. Torrence shared that the mission was to create a digital wallet where individuals could access personal credentials from their phones on demand. Students would save time and money by no longer having to request transcripts, gather paper certificates, or manage paper files. But, more importantly, this app would allow them to interact with employers regarding credentials for open positions and match learning credentials with job specifications and employers. This immediate access would revolutionize the way businesses recruit candidates, match skills to job requirements, and hire employees.

Dr. Torrence stated, "Industry and business partners really want a clear picture of what a candidate for a job can do, what they are prepared for, and how relevant the skills are to their needs. This signals a method to support those expectations and strengthens our relationships to further students' success."

Three of the approximately 100 Motlow State Mechatronics students who participated in the beta testing of the app shared their experiences with the group. Each student's story supported the usefulness of the app and the value in holding all of their certifications, skills, grades, and other credentials in one place immediately available to share with employers and potential employers.

Melissa Paz, Mechatronics faculty, stated, "When I was introducing the Metaversity app to the students in Mechatronics, I thought about all the certifications that I had earned in my career and where did I place those paper certifications. This app is so amazing that it matches your coursework and skills to job opportunities with the ability to send your resume to prospective employers with a few finger swipes; that sure beats all the typing I did in my day. I love the possibilities that Metaversity gives our students."

Motlow Students Jace Oliver, Helen Hayes, and Jill Holmes, each recounted experiences when their digital wallet helped them get an interview, get a job, or document job-related skills that turned into a raise. They also answered questions from the group supporting the movement into Phase II of development further extending the usefulness of the app.

Larry Flatt stated, "The vision for Metaversity is a leading-edge concept which will eventually benefit individuals at all education facilities whether large or small. With the recognition that micro-credentials, credentials, and certifications are an integral part of demonstrating competencies inside the academic process, there has arisen the need for a repository of all these things. With its completion, Metaversity is the answer."

Phase II includes plans to allow the digital wallet holder (DWH) to use the app to search for jobs on job boards such as Indeed, Handshake, ZipRecruiter, and others job search resources. An additional feature will allow, when authorized by the DWH, an employer access to credentials inside the individual's wallet to make a comparison of skills versus requirements required for each open position. Plans are for work on Phase 2 to begin in third quarter 2023 with testing scheduled for late 2023 and into 2024.

-end-

Cutline Metaversity 1: Motlow College Mechatronics Students Helen Hayes, Jace Oliver, and Jilliam Holmes presented feedback regarding the usefulness of the Metaversity app at a recent meeting at Motlow's Smyrna campus.

Cutline Metaversity 2: Mr. Larry Flatt, Executive Director of Motlow's Automation and Robotics Center, explains the process of creating the Metaversity app with industry and business partners to meeting attendees.

Unleashing the Power of Synergy: AI, Higher Education, and Social Justice (Part 1)

Introduction:

In the current milieu where technology is interwoven into the fabric of society, higher education institutions have a paramount role in cultivating and advancing innovation. Through strategic partnerships with business and industry organizations, and state departments, colleges and universities can be the linchpins that foster community advancement. The critical synergy lies within utilizing Generative Artificial Intelligence (AI) in supporting justice – involved individuals, youths in and young adults aging out of foster care, and those navigating collegiate recovery programs.

The power of Generative AI, through algorithms like GPT, has opened a new frontier in technology. The program can process and generate information at an unprecedented rate, adapting and evolving with use. We can envision ourselves, singularly or in groups, discussing thinking about thinking. I think of thinking as a patchwork of patterns and AI's ability to sift through, recognize, and subsequently reorient and reconnect disparate patterns through programming has always been intriguing. These capabilities can be harnessed in developing academic programs and workforce training programs that are responsive to the needs of the forthcoming list of target groups, skills gaps, and employer marketplaces. Further, our target groups have traditionally been identified by a myriad of markers from ethnicity and gender to socioeconomic status and age. Today, customized curated curricula and adaptive learning platforms, backed by AI, can provide learners and earners with resources that speak directly to their situations and learning styles. Let us take a snapshot at a different set of target groups; the justice – involved, at-risk youth, and students in collegiate recovery programs.

We support justice – involved humans. One of the most pressing opportunities facing our society is reintegration of justice – involved persons into the community. Institutions of higher education, in collaboration with business and industry organizations and state departments, can provide a lifeline for these individuals. We know that 95% of all who go behind the wall will return to our communities. Society may find it staggering to consider the actual economic ripples that are negated by recidivism rates. By offering academic and technical programs tailored to their needs and that of industry, our institutions empower justice – involved persons with skills and knowledge necessary to secure stable employment. More deeply is the humanity of it all because such partnerships can offer mentorship opportunities, counseling services, and access to community resources. Moreover, we can create and foster supportive environments for all to thrive.

We can further empower at – risk youths too. At- risk youths face numerous obstacles in social and workforce integration that hinder their educational attainment. Due to perception, lack of awareness, or living in a resource desert, opportunities can seem daunting. However, there are rich examples of empowering those who age out of foster care with the support of foster care alumni. Kids To Love, located in Huntsville, Alabama, is one such source of actionable implementation and sustainable growth. The transition from foster care to independent adulthood can be an unsettling experience for many young adults. Higher education partnerships can play a crucial role in creating link like chains and empower foster care alumni to pursue their educational, training, and career aspirations. By providing targeted support, including financial aid, academic guidance, and mental health resources, these partnerships can equip foster care alumni with the tools they need to succeed. Collaborations with local businesses and state departments also create opportunities for internships, apprenticeships, and job placement. Further, this enables these individuals to establish stable and fulfilling futures. One of our partners, Lee Marshall, the Founder and CEO of Kids to Love and KTECH, leads her creative team by constructing a space and culture that exemplifies supporting foster care alumni and more. This program needs to be replicated more broadly. Their ability to leverage emergent technology and skills building has set them apart to support young adults and foster care alumni who can then monetize their skills with earning power they can set aside.

Advancing community through collegiate recovery may also be ideal. The issue of substance abuse and addiction among college students is a pressing concern that demands our attention. Higher education institutions, in tandem with business and industry organizations and state departments, can lead the charge in addressing this opportunity. The creation of Collegiate Recovery Academies began just over a year or so ago, spearheaded by the foresight of the Tennessee Department of Mental Health and Substance Abuse Services. Lipscomb University launched the first 4 – year academy and Motlow State Community College launched the first 2 – year academy. Advocacy begins with awareness and community dialogue. By providing comprehensive support, including counseling, peer mentorship, and academic accommodations, these programs help students in recovery overcome obstacles and complete their education. Additionally, partnerships with community organizations and employers can foster a supportive environment for recovery and offer career pathways for individuals to rebuild their lives.

The plight of the justice – involved and at – risk youths aging out of foster care continues. Individuals face insurmountable barriers in integrating into society and the workforce. Stigmas, lack of support, and limited resources can hinder progress. Additionally, garnering the kind of network, rather than creating a network, takes time. Collegiate recovery programs, aimed at students dealing with addiction recovery, also face similar challenges. Higher education can bridge this gap by offering training and educational opportunities tailored to the unique circumstances of these populations. Justice – involved individuals often encounter barriers to education due to their criminal records or limited access to resources. However, with generative AI, we can create intelligent systems that offer personalized guidance, career exploration, and skills development. AI algorithms can analyze individual backgrounds and provide targeted recommendations for educational pathways, rehabilitation programs, and employment opportunities. This technology has the potential to empower justice – involved individuals to break the cycle of recidivism and build lives by further leveraging education as a tool of personal and professional advancement.

The ripple effect of community advancement when enhanced with AI is convergence. A space where institutions of higher education integrate Artificial Intelligence (AI) in collaboration with business and industry organizations, and state departments, the support for justice – involved persons, foster care alumni, and collegiate recovery becomes even more impactful. AI driven analytics can predict trends and optimize resource allocation for these target populations. This affords higher education and its communities of practice space to enhance the cycle of support, empowerment, and opportunity. Additionally, AI – based learning tools can create personalized skills-based learning and earning pathways. We have another point of entry now to cater to the unique needs and circumstances of everyone. This will be a set of SMART (Specific Measurable Achievable Relevant and Time – based) goals as a smart investment by the community in its most opportune target groups, coupled with AI, leads to even greater reduction in recidivism, increased employment rates, improved well – being, and exponential economic growth. We can put even more skilled persons back to work. The synergy of human endeavor and AI's capabilities amplifies the transformative power of these partnerships, creating an echoing wave of progress and not only impacting social change, but advance economic and community development.

Institutions of higher education stand at the fissure of revolutionizing community support through the convergence of human – centric partnerships and AI technology. By synergizing relationships with business, industry, and state departments, harnessing AI for individualized/tailored skills – based and academic programs, higher education can create an unparalleled web of opportunities. AI's analytics can help identify the cost of effective interventions and support networks. Moreover, AI powered chatbots and virtual assistants can provide constant support and mentorship to these populations. This integration of AI empowers these individuals to an unprecedented extent, making higher education institutions not just catalysts, but powerhouses for positive change. Our roles call for us to boldly embrace the boundless potential of AI – infused partnerships, we are not just paving, but illuminating the way for a future where every individual has the chance to rise, and communities do not just thrive, but flourish with innovation and human potential. By the way, what role will you play? Might we all aspire to the level of John B. Goodenough.

Beyond Synergy: Expanding Horizons with AI, Higher Education, and Social Advocacy (Part 2)

Having established the synergy between Generative AI, higher education, and strategic partnerships in part one, it is essential to explore how to broaden and sustain the impact. That is the purpose, impact. Advancements with and through emergent technologies are potentially growth engines for economies and areas otherwise excluded in the historical proximity of agrarian, industrial , and (older) technological scaling. Part II delves into establishing robust monitoring mechanisms, policy advocacy, and emergent global perspective. We have the opportunity in front of our local Tennessee community and its global partners to establish advanced monitoring and evaluation in concert with our citizenry. We can create synergy along open systems. We have already been providing "the" questions of ownership and design. The systems in Europe have already started to establish universal norms around AI policy, governance, and interworking/interlocking systems. We will do much of the same and encourage broad dialogue and engagement.

Our continuous feedback systems might be created to ensure the effectiveness of programs. A real-time feedback mechanism is necessary. So how do we do this? Utilizing Generative AI can analyze the data from multiple sources, giving valuable insights to our reviewers. In turn, this will also allow the collective "us" opportunity for timely interventions and adaptations. This is a power within the matrix, so to speak, where we have coded AI to seek while we can make determinations while looking at the possible, the plausible, and the potential flaws and problems simultaneously. Our critical eye is paramount in this Human Design element. We ought not simply turnover the keys to organizations, systems, governments, and complexes to AI. Moreover, our checks and balances will rely on programming, representative ethical programming, but also human intervention. The continuous feedback systems are our R&D and solutions.

The long-term impact analysis commingles with our ability to dynamically analyze the effects over time of educational programs on individual lives, communities, and funding. Perhaps this will be a mechanism to offset accessibility, poverty, and loss. We can leverage AI to track progress and identify areas where additional support or modifications are needed. I liken this recommendation to the work that has been ongoing with super/quantum computers for decades. The analysis can or could be equally robust under form. Consider education to employment as a starter. Additionally, we can co-create complex interwoven systems that produce granular and high-level data sets about long-term impact. Moreover, while we see generated data sets, our ability to intervene may increase under more observational circumstances. More bluntly, observe, orient, design, assess, and loop (OODA Loop).

Educational institutions should actively engage in policy advocacy. Collaborating with industry, state departments, and the local citizenry (our communities) can ensure that we will have lively civil discourse and democratic decisions that further support the educational and social integration of justice - involved individuals and at - risk youth. As an observation, we are all walking past youths at - risk and we need to be mindful of the pitfalls we have as society to only see sets of youths as at - risk. Would we as a society be better off if we supported the least of us as well as we support the best of us? Additionally, working towards reducing stigmas and discrimination, higher education institutions can lobby for reforms that facilitate the integration of marginalized populations into the workforce. These marginalized populations are, but not limited to, socioeconomic status, zip-code (education and resource deserts), veterans, literacy, age, etc. Obviously, there are a litany of marginalized groups not aforementioned, but certainly all important to advancing economies and meeting workforce shortages. Further, we must continue to consider how engagement with international policy advocacy potentially fosters an environment conducive to education, employment, and social integration. Our influence and voice can lend various perspectives to push learners and earners toward tomorrow. Collaboration may increase the likelihood that policies that support the educational and social integration of the justice involved and at - risk youth is seeded to flourish. Insomuch, there will exist a categorical review of legal and regulatory reforms. Working towards demystifying debts paid to society utilizing people first language to describe and engage with communities is a plus.

The next three points are about going glocal (global + local). Tennessee and a vast majority of the country are already glocal. We have foreign companies and subsidiaries employing many of our communities. Further, we must continue to consider how engagement with international policy advocacy potentially fosters an environment conducive to education, employment, and social integration. Our influence and voice can lend various perspectives to push learners and earners toward tomorrow. Collaboration may increase the likelihood that policies that support the educational and social integration of the justice involved and at - risk youth is seeded to flourish. Insomuch, there will exist a categorical review of legal and regulatory reforms. Working towards demystifying debts paid to society utilizing people first language to describe and engage with communities is a plus. We can use Generative AI to understand regional needs too. Perhaps development of curricula that resonates with dynamic populations worldwide could be aligned with bifurcated needs, both domestic and foreign.

We buy, sell, accept and in some cases share goods locally and internationally. Uncle Nearest and Jack Daniel spirits are good examples of locally sourced glocal products. Collaborative work with both of these companies continues to lead to greater innovation and collaboration for the betterment of our students. AI, rightly sized and purposefully used, will enhance these relationships and partnerships glocally. This kind of alignment leads to implementation of future technologies and innovations. The evolving technological advancements have ceased to “creep” and now literally “stream” into our life cycles of work, play, and hobby. We must stay abreast of and integrate innovative solutions to enhance the effectiveness and reach of training programs, both technical and durable skills - or as I have been sharing, meta-skills. These ideas may or may not lead to fostering a culture of innovation, but it is precisely what we may need to lean forward. Our ability to create an ecosystem that encourages applied innovation within educational institutions will create positive ripples. Applied research and development activities focused on addressing the challenges faced by marginalized populations helps all.

The progression beyond the initial synergy must be centered and anchored in resilience, comprehensive growth, and dynamic adaptability. Higher education institutions must remain alert and responsive, always seeking to enhance their offerings and services. As we continue to navigate this journey, we must remain committed to rigorous monitoring, influential policy advocacy, international collaboration, and the relentless pursuit of innovation. In the end, higher education, aligned with advanced technology and compassionate advocacy, can catalyze transformative generational change. It can redefine the future for millions of individuals, their families, and communities, who may have otherwise been left in the shadows of societal progress. The blending of technology and empathy can paint a new horizon, where no child, no family, no community is denied, irrespective of borders or societal standing. We continue to have opportunities to transcend. Let us all work towards an era of universal growth and empowerment, where the echoes of connected communities can be heard and felt across our townships, cities, regions, states, and nations, reaching out to every corner of the globe, profoundly impacting the lives of generations to come. We are literally planting trees, for which we may never sit under to enjoy their shade.

Digital Badging: From Novelty to Mainstream: Part I

The concept of digital badges emerged around 2010 as a novel way to credential skills and achievements in online learning environments. Early pioneers like Mozilla saw badges as a supplement to traditional degrees and certifications, allowing granular recognition of competencies gained through informal and self-directed learning.
In the decade since, digital badges have steadily gained traction. By 2023, over 300 organizations had issued open badges aligned to standards like Open Badges. Millions have earned badges from platforms like LinkedIn, Coursera and Udacity. Badges are no longer a novelty - they are now a mainstream mechanism for recognizing learning.

Several key developments account for the growing ubiquity of digital badges:

- Alignment with skills frameworks. Major employers like IBM and NASA have mapped their competency models to badge frameworks, enabling targeted credentialing tied to in-demand skills.
- Integration in learning platforms. Issuing open badges is now a standard feature in most LMS and MOOC platforms like Canvas and edX. This expanded access has fueled badge adoption.
- Focus on equity. Badges provide accessible credentials for those underserved by traditional education pathways due to cost, geography or discrimination. This mission resonates strongly today.
- Employer acceptance. More employers now see value in skills-based hiring supported by digital badges on resumes. Badges verify competencies directly relevant to jobs.
- COVID acceleration. The pandemic massively grew online learning and credentialing. Digital badges filled a key niche during this disruption.

Yet for all the progress, digital badges still occupy just a fraction of the enormous credentialing landscape. Tremendous potential remains to be unlocked in aligning badges to employment frameworks, integrating badges into human resources systems, and using badges to create equitable credentialing ecosystems.

Realizing this potential will require expanded collaboration between issuers, tech providers, employers, and workforce agencies. Thought leaders must continue advocating for skills-based, equitable credentialing while addressing valid concerns around quality and credibility.

The opportunity exists to move badges from a novelty model to the mainstream credential of the future. The need is clear. The technology exists. Forward-thinking leaders across education, government and industry can make it happen.

While badges have made great strides, most credentials today still come in the form of degrees and certifications from traditional educational institutions. But this is changing rapidly. More employers now recognize the need for skills-based hiring and see non-degree digital credentials like badges as a valuable talent signal.

The massive shift to remote work and online education spurred by COVID-19 has also accelerated the adoption of digital credentialing. Badges allow accessible, affordable recognition of skills gained through online learning.

Significant headwinds remain, however. Perceptions persist that badges lack academic rigor and quality assurance compared to traditional credentials. Additionally, widespread adoption is hindered by a lack of interoperability between badge platforms and human resources systems.

Tackling these challenges will require coordinated effort across sectors:

- Education providers should map badge frameworks to learning outcomes, career pathways, and equity goals. This alignment is key to credibility.
- Technology firms must make issuing, storing, displaying and verifying digital credentials seamless and secure. Blockchain solutions hold promise here.
- Employers should identify skills critical to success and work with issuers to develop aligned badge programs. Hiring and promotion processes can then incorporate badges.
- Workforce agencies can promote policies that expand access to skills-based hiring and credentialing. Funding and incentives can encourage badge adoption.

Realizing the badge potential will also require advocacy and education. Thought leaders must make the ethical case for skills-based, equitable credentialing and provide guidance on effective implementation.

With concerted effort across these fronts, digital badges could evolve from a fringe concept to the predominant credential of the future - one that unlocks opportunities for workers, employers, and underserved populations. The need and technology exist. Now is the time to unmuzzle badge advocates and fulfill the disruptive promise of this burgeoning ecosystem.

In just over a decade, digital badges have gone from a novel idea to a widely adopted credentialing mechanism. Millions have earned badges, and major organizations now issue them. Badges fill a vital niche in documenting the kinds of skills - both technical and soft - increasingly sought after in the modern workforce. They provide accessible credentials to populations underserved by traditional education pathways. Yet badges still occupy just a fraction of the overall credentialing landscape. Realizing their full disruptive potential requires commitment from stakeholders across sectors - education, technology, employers, government - to align badge frameworks to learning outcomes, career competencies, equity goals and hiring needs.

Advocates must continue making the ethical, economic and social case for skills-based credentialing while addressing concerns about quality assurance. With concerted effort, digital badges could evolve into the predominant credential of the 21st century workforce.

The need is clear. The technology exists. The time is now to unleash the disruptive potential of digital badges and create a more equitable, skills-based credentialing ecosystem that benefits workers, employers and society.

Realizing the full potential of digital badges will require overcoming key challenges:

- Perceptions of credibility - Badges must continue building acceptance through transparency, alignment with learning outcomes, and integration of quality assurance mechanisms.
- Interoperability - There is a need for technology standards and infrastructure that allow seamless badge issuing, storing, sharing and verification across platforms.
- Stakeholder alignment - Employers, issuers, tech firms, and policymakers must actively collaborate to map badges to competencies and career frameworks.
- Resistance to change - The perceived threat of disruption from alternative credentials like badges may meet institutional resistance. Strong ethical and economic cases for change are required.
- Equity gaps - Any badge ecosystem must proactively broaden access and recognize skills gained outside of formal educational pathways.

Meeting these challenges will hinge on forming strategic partnerships:

- Issuer collaboratives can jointly develop badge frameworks mapped to industry competency models and learning objectives. This boosts credibility.
- Partnerships between credentialing bodies, tech firms and blockchain providers can solve interoperability hurdles through improved infrastructure.
- Close coordination between employers, workforce agencies and issuers can embed digital badges into hiring, promotion and development processes.
- Cross-sector coalitions of credentialing innovators are needed to advocate for policy frameworks that support skills-based hiring and alternative credentials.

With a spirit of open collaboration and commitment to equitable credentialing, these partnerships can drive digital badge adoption while addressing legitimate concerns. Together, stakeholders have the power to fulfill the workforce disruption potential of this burgeoning movement.

Potential partnerships and strategies to drive continued adoption of digital badges:

- K-12 school districts should partner with badge issuers to develop programs recognizing competencies and “soft skills” critical for success in work and college but often overlooked in traditional grading. Badging extracurriculars like sports, arts, and service can expand access to credentials.
- Higher education institutions can work with industry groups and employers to map badge frameworks to college degrees and translate transcript data into meaningful skills credentials. This builds credibility and enhances career pathways.

- Professional associations should leverage their expertise in competency models and member needs to develop role-specific badge programs. This provides value to members while expanding recognition of skills gained through informal learning.
- Technology firms must partner with HR system providers to enable seamless integration and verification of digital credentials like badges within hiring and talent management workflows. Blockchain-based credential wallets have the potential to drive adoption here.
- Labor unions can negotiate to incorporate digital badges into the promotion, professional development and compensation structures of union workplaces. This unlocks badges' potential to recognize skill gains toward career advancement.
- Government workforce development agencies should fund pilot programs exploring skills-based hiring practices that utilize digital credentials like badges. Policy and funding incentives can catalyze adoption.

Through inspired partnerships across these sectors, digital badges can permeate credentialing ecosystems and fulfill their promise as the skill-based credential of the future. But collaboration and advocacy are key to overcoming inertia. The time to act is now. As Doug Belshaw and Laura Hilliger have recently posited, there needs to be continued advocacy for "open recognition for everyone."

Digital Badging and Broadening Perspectives on Digital Credentialing and AI: Part II

As the movement for digital credentials like badges gains steam, we must take care to consider key perspectives that will shape ethical implementation. Specifically, how can credentials provide value locally and globally while anticipating impacts of emerging technologies like AI? A few critical viewpoints stand out.

At the local level, badges must address on-the-ground realities within education systems and job markets. Issuers should partner with educators, employers and workforce agencies to make badges meaningful. For example, badges recognizing locally-valued skills could provide career pathways for those failed by traditional systems.

Nationally, credentials must align to policy frameworks like degree requirements, hiring practices and competency models. Consultation across sectors can enable policies supporting skills-based credentialing. For instance, badges recognizing military experience could assist transition to civilian roles.

Globally, credentials should enable transparency and portability across borders. A teacher earning instructional badges in one country could demonstrate pedagogical expertise elsewhere. Global standards around issuing and verifying digital credentials can enable this.

We must also get ahead of biases in AI and data-driven hiring algorithms that can perpetuate inequality. Credentials based on skills rather than arbitrary factors can help focus hiring on abilities. But conscious design is required to ensure credentialing data prevents rather than enables discrimination.

Finally, the ultimate goal should be empowering individuals to acquire credentials reflecting their evolving skills and interests. User-controlled credential wallets leveraging blockchain offer potential to shift agency to learners. But we must balance portability with institutional needs for verification.

Reconciling these varied perspectives will require substantive collaboration among issuers, tech firms, policymakers, employers and learners themselves. No single viewpoint should dominate. Ongoing dialogue and iteration will be key. One strategy is bridging micro-credentials like badges to established degree frameworks. Another is developing policy toolkits and incentives for skills-based hiring. We can also integrate ethical AI guidelines into credential system design.

By taking a broad view, digital credentials can simultaneously achieve local relevance, national alignment, global portability, AI ethics and individual empowerment. This conversation is just beginning. Through proactive partnership, we can guide credential innovation toward ethical and empowering ends.

We must also consider the viewpoint of marginalized populations who have faced systemic barriers to traditional credentialing. Digital badges have the potential to recognize skills and experiences overlooked by formal degrees and transcripts. But only if explicitly designed as on-ramps for the disadvantaged.

Issuing organizations should proactively partner with community colleges, nonprofits and workforce agencies focused on expanding economic opportunity. Co-designing credential frameworks that value skills from lived experience and informal learning is key.

Likewise, the perspective of small business owners and startup entrepreneurs should help shape digital credentials. Badges recognizing niche technical abilities, soft skills and experiences like apprenticeships can enable hiring in roles where degrees don't fit. Partnerships with chambers of commerce and economic development agencies can help surface small business needs.

Educators, too, have an important vantage on translating learning into credentials that facilitate career pathways. Teacher-led design of badges tied to K-12 and higher education outcomes can make credentials meaningful to the academic context. These exchange value with employers.

We must also anticipate the future perspective of students and young workers who will come of age expecting credentials reflecting their dynamic skills. User-centered digital credential wallets could shift agency to learners in managing credentials from diverse sources.

No one viewpoint should dominate as we evolve more equitable and empowering credentialing ecosystems. But proactively seeking diverse perspectives will ensure digital credentials adapt to the needs of local communities, disadvantaged populations, small businesses, educators and individuals.

An example of proactive collaboration is Motlow State Community College's new digital credentialing ecosystem. Motlow's Dynamic Skills Wallet, the Metaversity, issues blockchain-secured badges and certificates to students and community members reflecting technology competencies, soft skills and work experiences mapped to regional employer needs.

Key to this initiative was engagement across stakeholders. Regional industry partners provided critical input on high-demand skills to incorporate. Local non-profits helped shape credential frameworks to recognize skills gained outside college. Workforce agencies are aligning hiring incentives to credentials from the wallet.

Most importantly, Motlow learners control what credentials they share and with whom. This agency and portability empowers individuals to curate and convey their evolving skills capacities. By soliciting perspectives across industry, education, government and its own student community, Motlow State created an inclusive platform for skills-based credentialing aligned to local needs. This model shows the potential of broad collaboration to drive ethical and empowering digital credential innovation.

The Motlow State example highlights several key strategies for inclusive digital credentialing innovation:

- Proactively seek diverse perspectives from industry, community groups, workforce agencies, faculty and especially learners themselves. Cross-sector collaboration is key.
- Design credential frameworks around competencies and skills with transparent relevance to employment needs and career pathways. This builds value for all stakeholders.
- Incorporate both technical hard skills and interpersonal soft skills into credential taxonomy. Both are critical for career success.
- Enable learner agency through user-controlled credential wallets that facilitate portability and choice in sharing credentials. But allow verification mechanisms for employers.
- Map credentials to degree and certificate frameworks to maintain ties to formal education pathways where relevant.
- Actively use credentialing to broaden access and opportunities for non-traditional learners excluded from traditional degree pipelines.

By coming together across sectors and communities, we can steer emerging credentialing models toward inclusive and empowering end goals. Digital badges are just the beginning. With consistent dialogue and iteration, innovative credentialing systems can help build a more equitable society.

The perspectives we bring today will shape that future. Let us embrace this opportunity with wisdom, foresight and humanity.

HIATT - SPIVEY CENTER

The Future of Digital Credentials and Artificial Intelligence in Workforce Development: Part III

As our economy and society continue to be transformed by technological innovations like artificial intelligence and big data analytics, it is crucial that we consider how to best prepare the workforce of the future. An important part of this preparation will involve rethinking how we credential skills, knowledge, and experience through digital badges and verifiable credentials. To implement these systems effectively, we must take into account local, national, and global perspectives on workforce needs, while aiming toward shared goals of empowering learners and fostering a dynamic, skilled workforce.

At the local level, community colleges, trade schools, and local employers are ideally positioned to provide insights into the most in-demand skills and credentials for their region. Input from local stakeholders can help shape credentialing programs that are responsive to local labor market demands. For example, community colleges in regions with a strong healthcare sector may prioritize badges for skills in healthcare administration or medical technology.

Local perspectives examples:

- A healthcare skills badge developed through a partnership between a community college and local hospital system to meet demand for medical coders.
- A sustainable agriculture credential designed by a regional urban farming collaborative and issued to community members who complete their training program.

Nationally, policymakers and industry groups can take a broader view, identifying credentials that have currency across multiple industries and regions. National-level collaborations can also promote development of standards around issuing, earning, and verifying digital credentials. Groups like the American Council on Education have already begun leading efforts to map digital badges to college credit recommendations.

National perspectives examples:

- A digital literacy badge endorsed by the National Science Foundation and major tech companies that verifies baseline technology skills expected across industries.
- A hospitality service credential developed by a hotel industry association and recognized by member hotels, resorts, and restaurants across the country.

Global perspectives will also be key, as digital badges make skills visible across borders. The Open Badges standard developed by Mozilla and the Credential Transparency Alliance convened by the World Economic Forum represent early global efforts to build an interoperable credentialing ecosystem. More work is needed to define globally-recognized credentials while allowing for local variances.

Global perspectives examples:

- A multilingual communication badge based on the CEFR standard that uses AI-powered language assessment and is recognized across Europe.
- A digital marketing credential incorporating cross-cultural advertising skills, issued on blockchain to be verifiable across borders.

As we develop these new credentialing systems, we must consider who stands to benefit most from them. Learners should be empowered to earn credentials that represent their full range of competencies, opening doors to new learning and career opportunities. Similarly, employers need access to reliable signals of skills and knowledge when hiring. With thoughtful design, credentials can facilitate matching between worker skills and employer needs.

Empowering learners examples:

- A micro-credentialing program at a high school that allows students to accumulate career-related badges in areas like business, programming, and design.
- A platform where workers can compile all badges and credentials earned from multiple sources into a portable profile to share with employers.

The rise of artificial intelligence and machine learning will transform the workplace in ways we cannot fully anticipate. But these technologies also create opportunities to rethink how we prepare and credential the workforce. AI and big data can help calibrate credentialing systems to labor market demands in close to real-time. They can also power new modes of assessing complex skills. Rather than fearing displacement by AI, we can harness it to augment human potential.

Enhancing hiring examples:

- An AI screening tool that scans resumes and digital credential profiles to surface candidates with credentials matched to open positions.
- A virtual interview simulation that objectively assesses soft skills using behavior data and issues a verified diplomacy badge.

Achieving this future requires aligning disparate stakeholders toward shared goals: empowering lifelong learners, equipping workers with meaningful credentials, and building an agile workforce ready for the future of work. With open communication, partnerships, and a human-centric view, we can steer emerging credentials and AI toward democratizing economic opportunity. The future remains unwritten, but through cooperation and imagination we can author one that benefits us all.

Preparing the Workforce for the Electric Vehicle Revolution and Intersecting Digital Credentials and AI

The electric vehicle (EV) market is accelerating, with EVs expected to make up over 50% of new car sales by 2030. This profound shift brings immense opportunities along with workforce training challenges. How can regions like Southern Middle Tennessee capitalize on the EV transition while ensuring workers have needed skills? The Automation Robotics Training Center (ARTC) in McMinnville provides a model for workforce alignment.

Centrally located along I-24 and home to several major manufacturers, the McMinnville area is strategically positioned to become an EV and clean energy hub. The ARTC, a joint effort by Motlow State Community College and Tennessee College of Applied Technology McMinnville, offers specialized training in mechatronics, robotics, and automation. Programs like these that blend technical skills with hands-on learning are ideal preparation for the complexities of EV maintenance and manufacturing.

Critical will be engaging regional employers to understand their transition plans and future workforce needs. With many automotive jobs requiring new technical skills for EVs while retaining foundational mechanical and electrical knowledge, innovative credentialing approaches are needed. Apprenticeships integrating college credit allow workers to upskill efficiently. Stackable micro-credentials enable current staff to add EV expertise while maintaining productivity.

Partnerships between higher education, industry, and government can design credentialing pathways tailored to emerging roles like EV battery technicians and EV fleet managers. Tennessee is well-positioned to lead with its Drive Electric Tennessee initiative and national leadership in apprenticeships. Targeted state and federal funding can support more programs like the ARTC to be hubs of upskilling.

This transition is bigger than any single organization. Creating regional ecosystems that allow education, industry, and government to coordinate and share intelligence will best position the workforce for success. Open communication channels will allow responsive adjustments to meet needs. A shared vision for building both regional prosperity and sustainable mobility is key.

With thoughtful planning and collaboration, the move to EVs can usher new opportunities across Southern Middle Tennessee. The ARTC provides a strong foundation, with its integrative programming model and industry relationships. Expanding this approach will enable workers to access the technical training and credentialing needed to participate and excel in the EV economy. Proactive efforts today will assure the innovation and opportunity of this transformation are shared by all.

Beyond technical skills, the EV transition necessitates a mindset shift for workers and employers. For decades, the internal combustion engine powered the automotive industry. EV manufacturing and maintenance involves new technologies, processes, and even business models. A focus on continual learning is imperative.

Companies must provide ongoing training in EV technologies for employees to upskill. Apprenticeship programs, in-house training academies, and tuition assistance can enable this. Meanwhile, workers should be encouraged to adopt lifelong learning habits. Micro-credentials allow bite-sized learning pathways tailored to evolving needs.

The ARTC is well positioned to be a learning hub for the region. Programming could expand beyond students to support incumbent worker upskilling. Partnerships with employers can identify skills gaps and develop targeted training. Virtual and augmented reality can simulate hands-on EV experience at scale when physical equipment is limited.

Rather than a threat, automation and AI should be presented as tools to augment human work. Technicians need to know how to collaborate with robots and leverage data. Soft skills like communication, critical thinking and change management will only grow in importance alongside technical aptitude. Training in an interdisciplinary environment like the ARTC develops these holistic skills.

Transition brings uncertainty, but maintaining open dialogue between all stakeholders can ease anxieties. Employers should provide assurances that workforce development is a joint effort, with support resources available. Workers should clearly communicate their needs and concerns. Constructive collaboration will create mutual understanding and buy-in.

Equity and inclusion must be considered so opportunity is democratized. Intentional outreach and support for underrepresented groups in technical fields is key. Partnerships with local high schools can inspire diverse talent into EV careers. Ongoing training in implicit bias and inclusive hiring practices enables fairer mobility.

The path forward promises exciting innovations that will transform transportation sustainability. With planning, communication and collaboration, Middle Tennessee can lead this shift while ensuring economic mobility for all its workers. The ARTC provides a platform to bring together critical partners in industry, education and government around this common need.

AI and EV

As EV technologies advance, artificial intelligence and automation will transform vehicles and manufacturing. EVs rely heavily on software and have far more connected features than internal combustion vehicles. Self-driving technology is progressing rapidly. AI is also powering improvements in EV battery design, predictive maintenance, and intelligent charging infrastructure.

These AI advancements create opportunities to reinvent workforce training. Interactive simulations using VR/AR can provide immersive skill-building with various EV systems in a risk-free environment. AI tutors can offer personalized guidance and feedback for learners. For technicians, AI-assisted tools can enhance diagnostic capabilities and maintenance precision.

The ARTC is well positioned to incorporate AI into its programming for both students and incumbent workers. Partnerships with tech firms can provide access to leading AI tools. Curriculum can be designed around hands-on learning with AI-enabled EV test systems and prototypes. Working with intelligent technology directly builds critical experience.

It will be vital to have an ethical framework guiding the use of AI. Its integration into training and workplaces should emphasize augmenting human abilities rather than replacing jobs. Transparent and unbiased AI algorithms should be verified. Ongoing ethics education helps workers act responsibly. The ARTC can lead in promoting principled innovation.

Communication, adaptability and critical thinking skills take on greater importance to complement technical knowledge. Workers need to know how to collaborate effectively with AI systems. Curricula must emphasize the intersection of human and artificial intelligence. Hybrid online/in-person learning models allow efficient skill-building while cultivating teamwork.

Preparing Middle Tennessee for the AI-transformed future of EVs requires broad cooperation between industry, government, academia and workers. The ARTC's model of stackable credentials linked to real employer needs via collaborative design promises responsive and ethical training. With inclusion and innovation, the region can lead the electric and intelligent mobility revolution.

An important enabler for preparing the workforce for the AI-driven future of EVs is the use of digital credentials stored in virtual wallets. Platforms like Metaversity allow workers to collect and showcase credentials like badges, certificates and licenses in a portable profile. These can demonstrate competencies gained through training programs, professional experience, and assessments.

For EV maintenance technicians and manufacturing workers, digital credentials are ideal for displaying their evolving skill sets in areas like battery chemistry, power electronics, autonomous systems, simulation, and connected vehicle technologies. Granular micro-credentials allow step-by-step demonstration of proficiencies.

The ARTC is well positioned to issue digital credentials to students and incumbent workers that align with employer needs and industry standards. Their partnerships across higher education and industry enable tight integration. Credentials can be designed collaboratively then delivered through Metaversity.

This ecosystem provides benefits for learners, employers, and educators. Learners can accumulate credentials across formal and informal learning experiences while customizing their profile. Employers gain real-time visibility into candidate capabilities that are validated by trusted sources. Educators can track employment outcomes, adjust curricula, and expand offerings.

For continued success, the platform must prioritize transparency and interoperability. Financial or technical barriers to accessing the digital wallet should be minimized, along with biases in credentialing algorithms. Open standards will allow integration with other systems. Change management will assist stakeholders in smoothly transitioning.

As Middle Tennessee steers through the transformative EV and AI revolution, agile credentialing approaches will be critical for empowering its workforce. The ARTC can lead this new paradigm in collaboration with partners across industry, government and education. Digital credentialing ecosystems promise to democratize opportunity - but require cooperation to implement ethically at scale.

Institutional research professionals and campus wide relationships: influence across higher education

Institutional research (IR) professionals play a vital role in providing data and analysis to inform strategic decisions at colleges and universities. However, the position of the IR office can often be isolated from senior leadership. Through research, the following themes are seemingly consistent when developing strong working relationships and influence with the President's Office; it is critical for IR professionals to fully contribute to institutional effectiveness.

One effective strategy is to align IR projects and priorities with the strategic goals articulated by the President and/or board of trustees. For example, if increasing student retention and graduation rates is a priority, the IR Office could proactively analyze trends and patterns in these metrics over time, broken down by academic programs and student demographics. Presenting findings and recommendations to the President's leadership team shows how IR can directly inform efforts to improve outcomes in line with institutional goals.

It is also important for IR professionals to establish open communication channels with the President's Office outside of formal meetings and reports. Informally checking in on key issues and emerging needs provides an opportunity to offer IR's expertise. I suggest effectively positioning IR as an objective and credible "Information and Insight Resource" that builds trust and influence with faculty and staff across the organization. Maintaining professionalism, confidentiality, and tact is crucial when interacting closely with the President's Office. IR professionals must avoid getting drawn into campus politics or voicing unsolicited opinions on management issues outside the scope of IR's role. Demonstrating discretion and neutrality will earn respect from institutional leadership.

In today's data-driven climate, the expertise of IR is more valuable than ever for higher education leadership. Thoughtfully engaging with the President's Office, aligning with strategic priorities, and providing timely and relevant insights will help IR professionals maximize their impact on institutional effectiveness with faculty and staff across the organization. In addition to aligning IR work with institutional goals, it is also important to tailor reports and presentations to the informational needs of the President and other senior leaders. As I have observed, executives often prefer high-level data summaries that focus on key trends, benchmarks, and recommendations. Dense statistical reports may be better suited for IR websites or archives.

When given the opportunity to present to the President's Office, IR professionals should highlight data that answers pressing questions or surface issues requiring leadership attention. This may require requesting input ahead of time on the most useful areas to cover. Clear and concise visualizations that convey insights "at a glance" are invaluable for busy higher education leaders. Might I suggest establishing an "early warning system" where IR regularly provides the President's Office with environmental scanning reports about emerging issues and developments that could impact the institution. This proactive approach positions IR as an objective, forward-looking resource, not just a historical data provider.

Institutions of higher education are complex organizations with many competing priorities and stakeholders. As we all should recognize, IR professionals must sometimes frame recommendations carefully to align with political realities on campus. Savvy IR leaders understand the motivation of different leaders and departments and present data insights in ways that constructively inform realistic next steps. Establishing credibility and relevance with the administration takes political acumen in addition to technical expertise.

By focusing on the highest-priority information needs of the President's Office, communicating professionally and discreetly, and providing politically prudent recommendations, institutional research professionals can maximize their influence and contribute meaningfully to data-informed leadership and strategic planning. These best practices from expert leaders can guide IR Offices in enhancing their vital role.

Perhaps these are some effective strategies institutional research professionals can use to increase engagement and collaboration campus-wide:

- Host open forums to solicit input on IR priorities and projects from faculty, students, and staff. This promotes transparency and buy-in.
- Establish an IR users group of power users from academics, admissions, finance, etc. to get feedback on reports and analytics.
- Create an IR newsletter or blog to regularly share data updates, trends, and useful visualizations with the campus community.
- Offer workshops and training for departments on constructing surveys, analyzing data, and using IR reporting tools. Empower stakeholders to engage directly with data.
- Partner with academic departments, student affairs, and faculty researchers on analytics relevant to their work. Co-present findings at campus conferences.
- Develop a catalog of standard IR reports and analytics available on demand for end users across campus. Market this resource.
- Publish an annual IR Performance Report showcasing key projects, findings, and recommendations over the past year.
- Advocate for enterprise data governance policies that promote data accuracy, consistency, security, and availability for reporting.
- Create virtual data dashboards that unite disparate campus data sources into visualizations that address cross-functional concerns and questions.

The goal is to position IR as an approachable, transparent resource for the entire institution. Proactive outreach and stakeholder education enables IR to drive a culture of data-informed planning and decision making campus-wide. It is through the review, reflection, and discussion of the meaning of data that we can advance our support of students, faculty, staff, and communities.

Looking towards the future, institutional research professionals in higher education will play an even more vital role as data-driven decision-making becomes increasingly integral to the success of institutions. Here are some potential developments and challenges they might face:

1. Advanced Analytics: With the advent of advanced data analytics and artificial intelligence, institutional research professionals will have access to more sophisticated tools to analyze and interpret data, providing deeper insights into student behavior, retention, and performance.

2. Predictive Modeling: Utilizing predictive modeling, research professionals can forecast enrollment trends, student success rates, and financial outcomes, allowing institutions to proactively address challenges and opportunities.

3. Personalized Learning: Data-driven insights will enable personalized learning experiences tailored to individual students, enhancing student engagement and outcomes.

4. Big Data Integration: Institutional research professionals will need to navigate the complexities of integrating vast amounts of data from various sources while ensuring data security and privacy.

5. Emphasis on Equity: There will be a growing focus on using data to identify and address disparities in student outcomes, aiming to ensure equity and inclusivity in higher education.

6. Data Ethics: As the use of data becomes more prevalent, research professionals must be vigilant about ethical considerations, data transparency, and responsible data use.

7. Emerging Technologies: The rise of new technologies like blockchain and augmented reality may impact data collection and how institutions leverage research findings.

8. Interdisciplinary Collaboration: Institutional research professionals may need to collaborate more closely with faculty, administrators, and other stakeholders to address complex challenges in higher education.

9. Real-time Insights: The demand for real-time data and analytics will increase, enabling quicker responses to emerging issues and opportunities.

10. Remote Data Access: With the growth of remote work and virtual collaboration, research professionals may need to adapt to accessing and analyzing data from various locations securely.

Overall, the future for institutional research professionals is promising, with their expertise being sought after to shape data-informed policies, improve student outcomes, and guide higher education institutions toward greater success. However, they will need to continually upskill, embrace new technologies, and navigate ethical considerations to remain at the forefront of this evolving landscape. I am extremely interested to see the impact of emergent software and generative AI in this space as a teaching and innovation tool for the IT professional.

The Rise of AI in Higher Education: Boon or Bane for Student Success?

The emergence of artificial intelligence (AI) presents both opportunities and challenges for higher education. As an educational futurist, I am simultaneously invigorated and concerned by the rapid advancement of AI and its potential impact on students, those who live on the margins, and our collective communities. I harbor no undue ideas that stream doom nor gloom, however, I simply hope to situate a continued dialogue affixed to the constant need for regulatory oversight. Although we will continue to explore a myriad of subjects in various musings, the purposes are probing, applied research-centered with human centered design at its core. Emergent technology is no more perfect than we are as a species. Emergent technology is no more biased or unbiased than we are as daily interlopers on the planet. Emergent technology is another form of culture sound bite which acknowledges our beauty, but also our grotesqueness. Let's keep peeling back our zeros and ones for full discovery of a more permanent united center. I'll not remain optimistic for perfection, but I will remain an optimist of the needs of humans to need untethered linkages to one another. More simply, humans will forever need humans, but ethical AI offers incalculable value to improve the human condition.

On one hand, AI has the power to transform learning in profoundly positive ways. AI tutoring systems can provide customized support to each student, adapting in real-time to their strengths and weaknesses. Chatbots equipped with natural language processing can answer simple questions and free up faculty and staff for more meaningful interactions. Human to human interactions center contextual learning too. Automated writing evaluation tools can provide students with instant feedback, allowing them to improve their skills efficiently. The ability to make good better, better great, and take great to excellence is plausible. Framing the painting does not always have to be the last act of excellent art.

AI also holds great promise for improving student retention and graduation rates, perennial challenges facing colleges and universities. By analyzing vast amounts of data, AI can identify at-risk students early and connect them to targeted resources. Tailored AI advising systems can guide students in course selection and career planning, keeping them on track for timely completion. Enhanced learner analytics empower institutions to better understand obstacles to persistence and develop evidence-based interventions.

However, we must also remain cognizant of the ethical and social risks posed by the integration of AI in education. If institutions become over-reliant on AI for advising, students may feel disconnected and lose access to crucial human mentoring. Automated proctoring and writing evaluation raise valid concerns about privacy, bias, and fairness. Poorly implemented AI could also reinforce inequities if under-resourced students lack access to the latest tools and technologies.

As an educational futurist, I believe we must embrace the benefits of AI while also carefully examining its dangers. Students, especially those from disadvantaged backgrounds, should participate in the development and governance of AI tools to ensure they empower, rather than marginalize. Representative examples of AI discounting or not recognizing marginalized groups are abound. We need only ensure we exceed the limits of imaginative engineers and provide replicable input that emboldens all who will wield access to AI. We need critical perspectives on algorithmic bias and thoughtful frameworks for AI ethics in teaching and learning. And faculty require support in thoughtfully integrating AI in their pedagogy and curriculum. We have an opportunity to flush AI interoperable with holistic representative samples that span age, ethnicity, class, gender, etc. Consider all the representative census data and sew it together for good intentional use and we have a start. We would be able to pinpoint student needs based on more factors - environmental being one of them. Interesting to consider and even more interesting to apply. Success is as much about finishing the tasks as it is tied to the condition in which completion occurs.

The rise of AI presents a monumental opportunity to advance student success. But we must remain vigilant stewards, guiding its development in service of equity and human dignity. Only through inclusive innovation and ongoing ethical reflection can we harness the full power of AI to help support human ingenuity.

Here are examples of how AI could positively impact student success and institutional outcomes:

1. AI identifying at-risk students.
2. An AI system analyzes academic, demographic, and engagement data to flag students in danger of failing or dropping out. Early intervention connects students to tutoring, advising, financial aid, or other support. This could increase retention and graduation rates.
3. AI advising systems.
4. Chatbots and intelligent software provide customized course recommendations and degree planning based on a student's major, academic record, and career goals. This personalized guidance keeps students on track to graduate on time.
5. AI enhanced learner analytics.
6. Dashboards give faculty and advisors an early warning system to identify gaps in student learning. They can then adjust their teaching methods or offer targeted student support. This data-driven approach improves pedagogy and student academic achievement.

Here are potential consequences associated with overreliance on AI in education:

1. AI overreliance for advising students.
2. Students may feel disconnected from human mentors and the college experience.
3. Overdependence on algorithms can limit exploration and serendipitous learning.

4. Lack of nuanced human judgment in advising could lead to inappropriate or inadequate recommendations.
5. AI proctoring.
6. Privacy concerns around data collection during remote proctoring.
7. Potential for bias in automated test grading if the algorithms are not properly audited.
8. Limitations in AI's ability to accurately interpret complex human behaviors and emotions.
9. AI reinforcement of inequity, fairness, and bias.
10. Algorithms trained on biased datasets can perpetuate discrimination against minorities.
11. Lack of access to the latest AI technologies could widen achievement gaps.
12. Automation of administrative tasks could lead to loss of important student support jobs.
13. Students from marginalized communities may not have a voice in AI tool development.

Here are examples of thoughtful AI integration in curriculum, pedagogy, andragogy, and credentialing:

1. Curriculum.
2. AI collaboratively develops personalized learning pathways based on a student's strengths, needs and career goals.
3. Courses leverage AI to enhance creativity and critical thinking rather than replace human activities.
4. Pedagogy/Andragogy.
5. Faculty receive training to thoughtfully integrate AI tools that amplify (not automate) teaching.
6. Learner data helps instructors identify gaps, but human judgment drives interventions.
7. Credentialing.
8. Institutions use AI-enabled badges, skills certificates and microcredentials to expand access.
9. AI assists human evaluators in assessing competencies but final decisions involve human review.
10. Algorithms are continuously audited for bias to uphold fair credentialing standards.

The key is adopting AI in ways that center equity, ethics and meaningful human direction. AI should not drive the educational mission but rather enhance the critical thinking and social development at the heart of student success. The current iterative is to construct a system or interoperable shatters that allow for all learners and earners to insert their earned skills into portable digital credential wallets. Ai enhances this ability, our ability to support student success even further.

MOTLOW STATE COMMUNITY COLLEGE
FAYETTEVILLE CENTER

The Now of Work: New Collar Skills, Accessibility, and Economic Vitality Across America

The constant evolutionary landscape of the American Workforce has new collar skills at its core. The significance of this "skill cornerstone" is betwixt fluid and situated economies linked to topography and demography. To clarify, the fluid nature of work conjures up linkable dynamics due to the continued variance of what optimization and cost savings may look like for local, regional, and national employers. Think distribution centers and the ties to logistics and supply chains, but also the context of any form of digitized/hybridized "work from home" options. The situated economies are within our nurseries, dairy-beef-swine operations, and other table staples grown and harvested based on location across our nation. Obviously, without mentioning the builders of our nation in the construction – paving industries, financial-tech, and highly skilled tradesmen/women need to also correlate with first responders, healthcare, and hospitality – tourism – culinary – spirits industries, we would be short-sighted to exclude their importance. The new skills, situated at the nexus of technology, critical thinking, and creative problem-solving drive the next waves of economic development. This article seeks only to color the exploration of the imperative role of new-collar skills in employment, the essence of making training and learning accessible, and the ripple effects of innovation in revitalizing micro-metro and small-town rural economies.

The centrality of new-collar skills contrasts with the traditional white-collar or blue-collar classifications. The new-collar jobs demand a unique blend of technical aptitude and adaptive competence. At Motlow State Community College, we have developed specialized training programs in partnerships with 128 partners over the last 18 months. We are doing what all institutions that teach and train do, meeting the pace of the demand of our industry, business, and community partners. In partnership with learning platform providers like Microsoft and Google, or simulated training leveraging extended training tools like augmented reality and AI, we continue to innovate and develop the workforce. We have accounted for extended training of first responders in our AEMT/EMT programs utilizing some of the latest simulated training tools. We believe that this provides our graduates with more than hands-on, but proactively engages them in potentially "high stress" awareness simulations that better prepare them for the field. Simultaneously, we are providing tools for them to map their way through and to stronger employment options. Furthering our work across the intersections of new skill environments, cyber, aviation, and data analytic conversations are on the tips of our tongues too. Our existing and new programs enlist a capable and passionate group of faculties eager to prepare today's workforce. For example, use of advanced teaching and learning tools, to include, but not limited to AI, continues to be an organic extension in foundational areas like Science and Mathematics. Our Academic Resource Center, a space for faculty development, is growing and thriving. We are building upon the baselines that were before us.

Our growing partnerships will continue to yield impactful platforms for those we support and serve. Data analytics, dispositions, and skill alignment with current and emerging industries will continue to be a shared focus. We will continue to make strides in creating data-sharing platforms, which seamlessly interconnect educational institutions and employers. The phase one success of our omni-project, where students get real time insights into the market demands for new-collar skills, positions our students for success, now and well into the future.

Accessible learning is a democratic imperative. At the heart of training for these new opportunities lies the ethical obligation to make such learning and training accessible. Motlow State has extended its partnerships to launch courses in not only emergent, but fields of need. The aim is to break down barriers that often hinder skill development among marginalized communities. Partner contributions facilitate collaborations between educational and industry leaders to customize training solutions that are inclusive and affordable. The focus, create pathways that empower every individual to access upward mobility imagining beyond innovation towards application and amplification. The way we do anything, is the way we will do everything rings true.

Innovation and regional economic revival do not just flourish in urban centers; it is also revitalizing smaller micro-metro and small-town rural areas. Take, for example, the town of McMinnville, Tennessee. Motlow State's partnership with local manufacturers has led to workforce upskilling, subsequently attracting further investment in advanced manufacturing within the county and across our regional footprint. We continue to further our investments with Tennessee State University with smart agriculture. We want to continue to empower our rural communities to leverage technology for sustainable farming. These projects contribute significantly to local economies, turning them into pockets of vibrant activity.

Tourism, as Motlow State is within the trail head of Tennessee's Whisky Trail, is also receiving an innovation-led boost. Motlow State has developed a micro-credential and degree pathway for distilling. Further, the partnership between Uncle Nearest, Jack Daniel, and Motlow State, beginning in Fall of 2024, will garner additional opportunities for our students and entrepreneurs. Leveraging our innovation, The Uncle Nearest Distilling Academy will be an exemplar of our continued efforts to tailor programs to unique needs of small-town rural economies, maturing alongside them as engines of impact. On a similar note, our continued work with Brighthive will be instrumental in using the data to improve the experiences of those who visit our communities. We trust that approaches like these will uplift the local and regional economic landscapes.

In conclusion, this is an era of rapid change and development for Tennesseans. The vitality of new-collar skills, the democratization of learning, training, and innovation cannot be overstated. Together, they form a triad that has the potential to reshape not just individual lives, but entire communities. I believe we can scale these approaches and secure brighter futures for all invested and involved. Our collaborative efforts at Motlow

State Community College, in association with DXtera, Brighthive, and the Learning Economy Foundation, are more than just institutional initiatives. They are a manifestation of our collective vision for a future where prosperity and opportunity are widespread and enduring. As we forge ahead, let us all remember that the horizon of possibilities is as expansive as our willingness to venture into the unknown. It is a journey worth taking, for it holds the promise of a more accessible and dynamic America. We are and always have been, stronger together!

MARYLOU APPLE
SCIENCE-TECHNOLOGY-ALLIED HEALTH
MOTLOW
STATE

Navigating the Future: The Vital Role of Non-Linear Pathways in Micro-Credentialing and Stackable Credentials

In today's rapidly evolving job market, the concept of a linear career path has become increasingly obsolete. The traditional notion of graduating from high school or college, securing a stable job, and steadily climbing the corporate ladder is no longer the norm. Instead, we find ourselves in the midst of a new collar job skill-based economy, where adaptability and continuous learning serve as attributes key to success. Employment advancement can now be situated in prior learning and self-assertion for continued earning.

As we navigate this new landscape, one of the most crucial strategies for career advancement and personal growth is the utilization of non-linear pathways. Micro-credentialing and stackable credentials are to be levers. Pulling these levers in the pursuit of the generational building blocks necessary for today and the future. Micro-credentials to stackable credentials to bundled credentials will earn learners employment and continuous growth of their wages. These innovative approaches offer individuals the flexibility to acquire relevant skills and knowledge incrementally. Additionally, they align perfectly with the demands of the modern workforce. The workforce expectations will continue to evolve and this evolution does not posit the negating of degrees. Although we, Higher Education, hear the whispers of value and understand that inherent value does not make the option of training unviable, skills do pay the bills. The advanced skills will be more valuable as learners progress within and outside of what "traditional" employment has looked like in the past.

Micro-Credentialing are the building blocks of expertise in an economy calling for portable skill verification sans self assertion. Moreover, micro-credentialing involves the pursuit of short, focused courses or certifications that provide specific skills or knowledge in a particular area. These hyper impactful bite-sized learning experiences are designed to be accessible, practical, and immediately applicable to real-world challenges. This approach is not new, just more expected and accepted as it fits the model of today's culture of accelerated preparation and completion. "Chunk-able" offerings for individuals provide the opportunity to upskill or reskill in a cost-effective efficient manner. Decreasing completion time and adhering to the expectations of rigor academically and quality via workforce training is important. Community Colleges continue to develop work-ready graduates.

In the context of our ever-changing job market, micro-credentialing serves as the building blocks of expertise. It allows individuals to adapt, pivot, and further their careers with the alignment of stackable micro-credentials and traditional educational pathways. Whether it's mastering a new software tool, gaining proficiency in data analysis, or becoming an expert in a specialized field, micro-credentials offer the means to stay com-

petitive and relevant.
Our continued approach to stackable credentials is tethered to the opportunity to create a mosaic of skills. Stackable credentials take the concept of micro-credentialing a step further by enabling individuals to accumulate multiple certifications over time. We might consider it as an avenue to creating a tapestry of skills and qualifications that uniquely represent learner expertise. This approach empowers individuals to customize their learning journey and career trajectory.

In a world where employers increasingly value skills and competencies over formal degrees, stackable credentials offer a tangible way to showcase the learner's abilities. Whether entering the workforce for the first time, changing careers, or seeking advancement in a current job, the ability to stack credentials gives learners a competitive edge. It allows the curation of a portfolio of qualifications that directly align with industry needs and long term career goals.
We must continue to adapt to the "new collar" job skill based economy. This is simply another opportunity for our innovation to take root. New collar job skill-based economies are characterized by the emphasis on skills, not just degrees. Employers are looking for candidates who can hit the ground running, solve complex problems, and adapt to rapidly changing technologies. This shift in focus from qualifications to competencies necessitates a non-linear approach to education and skill development. We don't have to annex one approach to dynamically meet an emergent option. Higher Education can do both and more!

As a parent, community member, and part of an institutional leadership matrix, I am committed to providing educational and training opportunities that align with this evolving paradigm. We recognize the importance of micro-credentialing and stackable credentials in preparing our students for success in the new collar job market. Our programs are designed to be flexible, accessible, and responsive to the needs of both traditional and non-traditional learners. We have a cadre of faculty committed to strong and centered instructional methodologies and brave enough to also embrace advanced technology appropriately with care. These are strengths and benefits of a progressive subject matter expertise within the inner and exterior collaborators apart of our Academic Resource Center (ARC).

In conclusion, the importance of non-linear pathways in micro-credentialing and stackable credentials cannot be overstated. In a world where the only constant is change, these aforementioned strategies empower individuals. We want all to take control of their careers, adapt to the demands of the job market, and thrive in the new collar job skill-based economy. It is our collective responsibility to embrace these innovative approaches to education and ensure that every individual has the opportunity to unlock their full potential. We will continue to structure our learning pathways, strategic planning, and organizational needs for the advancements, not only for our students and employers, but our institutional community of learners and doers as well. We are and always will be as great or good as the least skilled or informed of us. We choose to support leading from wherever you are within our organization and community. We trust that this aims at our set targets and pinpoints where our efforts can best leverage continued collaboration for the success of ourselves and our communities.

Enhancing Credit Mobility for Future Workforce: A Strategic Approach in the Age of Accelerated Learning and Portable Credentials

In the previous essay, “The Now of Work: New Collar Skills, Accessibility, and Economic Vitality Across America,” we discussed the evolving landscape of the American Workforce. The foreshadowed emphasis highlighted the critical role of new-collar skills in driving economic and technological development. Where we once, and in some statuses continue to, segment the use of theoretical underpinnings and the applicable for its immediate impact, we must move beyond those inherent conclusions. This essay aims to expand upon the previous vision, one that focuses on the “how to” enhance credit mobility for learners. Moreover, we must also analyze with assertiveness the pivotal role of state policy makers and the strategies employed for expanding “approval” of previously acquired competencies in this rapidly changing era.

Enhancing credit mobility for learners is not new. When a local economy needs workers, it is twofold, we have long fashioned the necessary and desired “curricula/program” to deliver the skilled laborer or operator necessitated. The concept of credit mobility is central to the democratization of education, especially in new-collar fields. Consider the explosiveness related to new credential programs asserting how to learn prompt engineering for AI as an example. Amplification of learner success, wafts through the air like a cool breeze on a hot Tennessee summer night, burbling throughout educational institutions adopting flexible credit transfer systems. It is faint and it is an excited whisper, but we want to speak up and even yell to us it’s here. Otherwise, we might not pay attention to the obvious until we are sweat soaked and feigning deafness. There are instances and examples of the work in progress. The sunsetting program at the Western Interstate Commission for Higher Education’s Interstate Passport Program allows students to transfer lower-division general education credits seamlessly across member institutions https://www.wiche.edu/resources/interstate-passport-program-will-sunset-at-end-of-2023/. Similarly, the SUNY system in New York has successfully implemented a comprehensive credit transfer system, ensuring students retain maximum credits when moving between institutions https://system.suny.edu/academic-affairs/student-mobility/. The aforementioned speaks to the issue of credit mobility, but general education courses may not lead to a more skilled workforce in areas of technological advancement. We will keep seeking to balance these areas of emphasis. The California Association Degree for Transfer (ADT) Program guarantees students who earn an associate degree a saved spot at a California State University https://www.cccco.edu/Students/Transfer. I, like you, really like guarantees of most sorts and this selection process bundles learning accessibly porting students into their next learning environment. This initiative provides a clear and streamlined pathway for students, ensuring their credits are not, lost or tossed, in the transition from community college to university. I would posit that this could be the same kind of credit equity between technical colleges, community colleges and universities, for example, the East Tennessee State University Dual Degree RN to BSN Nursing Program pathway https://www.etsu.edu/nursing/undergrad/dual_degree_

rn_bsn.php. The European Credit Transfer and Accumulation System (ECTS) is a system, widely used in European higher education, which allows for the transfer of credits across institutions within the European Higher Education Area https://education.ec.europa.eu/education-levels/higher-education/inclusive-and-connected-higher-education/european-credit-transfer-and-accumulation-system. This is a model that exemplifies how a standardized credit system can facilitate international student mobility, offering a model like systems in the U.S. Moreover, it is important to remember that approval of transfer credit is different from acknowledging competency in a specific academic area.

The catalyst for broad impactful change rests with informed State policymakers and their teams. State policymakers play a crucial role in creating environments conducive to credit mobility. Policies such as statewide articulation agreements, as seen in Florida's Statewide Articulation Agreement, ensure that credits earned at any public post-secondary institution are transferable within the state. Moreover, initiatives like the Texas Higher education Coordinating Board's Fields of Study curricula lay out course sequences that are universally transferrable within the state, providing clear pathways for students. There are clear branches for additional legislative catalysts that might further spur acceleration. Dual enrollment, which just under a decade ago been unembraced, now reflects the plausible for many higher education and LEA partner-collaborations. Most recently, the Tennessee General Assembly focused efforts of streamlining opportunity for the Tennessee Colleges of Applied Technology and LEA dual enrollment pathways beginning in the 9th grade https://legiscan.com/TN/bill/SB2370/2021.

The next gathering of Tennessee's legislative body, will involve entertaining the option for 10th grade students to fully take advantage of dual enrollment at the states Community Colleges, furthering the impact and expanding much needed access. Further examples are easily located in the state of Minnesota, where their Postsecondary Enrollment Options program is a successful model that allows high school students to take college courses for credit, easing their transition into higher education. For those who operate within these spaces institutionally or via policy review, these exemplars are probably nothing new. The ability to replicate and scale models that work would be new. Humans learn. Humans train to enhance their learning. Humans build systems. Humans should build systems that are accessible and scalable, but above all else, systems should be effective and efficient above all else.. This leads to my last point of this focal area of what could serve as catalysts. The development of a Universally Integrated System (UIS), one loaded with statewide, nationwide, and localized integrated comprehensive data sets that open the superhighway of clarity from a "single pane of glass." Implementing a comprehensive data system that tracks student progress and credit accumulation across institutions can greatly aid in credit transfer. Such systems can provide insights for policy adjustments and identify barriers in credit mobility. The University of Texas System's data-driven initiatives offer a benchmark in this area. Further, the work conducted by the Education Strategy Group (ESG) also pushes toward solutions as they work with systems of higher education across the nation. ESG most notably supports needed dialogue between states like Colorado, Louisiana, Maryland, Ohio, Tennessee, and Washington. The states are, or moving toward, strengthening their credit mobility pathways. The recognition of the challenges of credit transfer in the U.S is more related to the vast differences in academic rigor, material covered, and competitive learning environments.

We can improve credit mobility. To improve credit mobility, we must embrace technology and innovative practices with more speed. For instance, blockchain technology can be leveraged to create secure, immutable, academic records, thus facilitating the transfer of credits and credentials. When we know and fail to act, or slow down advancement for the oddity of intellectual ejaculation, we all lose. The Massachusetts Institute of Technology's pilot program on blockchain-based education models, such as those implemented by Western Governors University, enable credit transfers based on skills and knowledge, rather than traditional credit hours. What would happen if we all acquiesce to flexible stretching instead of wooden spoons? We are more malleable than we give ourselves credit for or recognize. When we declutter, we see the example of the National Student Clearinghouse Transcripts Service. In the United States, The National Student Clearinghouse offers electronic transcript exchange services. The system streamlines the process of transferring credits between institutions, making it faster and more efficient. Who doesn't want effectiveness and efficiency? This approach aids in credit mobility. Additionally, the Bologna Process is an international example. The Bologna Process in Europe seeks to frame the creation of a more coherent higher education area. It focuses on standardizing degree structures, quality assurance, and the recognition of qualifications and periods of study. This process has significantly enhanced student mobility across European countries and serves as a model for global initiatives in education. These examples from both globally and the United States illustrate the dynamic strategies and initiatives to enhance credit mobility. They showcase how policy makers can be instrumental in fostering an educational environment that supports fluid and efficient credit transfer. Ultimately, the benefactor will be learners who, in navigating their educational and professional journeys, become even more likely to succeed.

We are in an era of hyper-awareness, hyper-stimuli, and creating computing that moves us closer to hyper-omnipresence – what will it be like to be everywhere? I suppose that could be another discussion for another time. I digress, that in an era of accelerated learning and portable credentials, it is a necessary imperative to re-evaluate traditional educational models. Are enough of us, brain trusts, going beyond asking questions, but seeking solutions? Collaborations between educational institutions, industry partners, and policymakers are essential. Currently, our liaison collaboration with the Learning Economy Foundation and DXtera Institute works to connect and build upon their existing efforts of creating education with career pathways through data and open standards. This is a step towards furthering such collaborations that can establish a universally integrated knowledge platform, and ensure that education is not only accessible, but also relevant and responsive to the needs of the workforce. The vision of a dynamic and accessible American workforce is not only attainable, but necessary for our collective future, would you agree? By focusing on enhancing credit mobility, involving state policymakers in creating advanced conditions, and adopting innovative methods. This ensures that education remains a powerful tool for economic vitality and individual empowerment. As we continue to push the boundaries of what is possible in education and workforce development, let us embrace the spirit of collaboration and innovation that is defining the currency of this new era.

CLAYTON-GLASS LIBRARY
MOTLOW STATE

Navigating the AI Evolution in Higher Education: Progress, Challenges, and Future Directions

Since the initial exploration of AI's potential in higher education, there has been a significant evolution in its acknowledgment, application, and impact. We hear the cultural acceptance and criticism across riveting dialogue between pundits, politicians, and private citizens. Organizations embrace its efficiency and speed, while also fumbling through methods to assert recognition and alignment of ethical use. Originally, the focus of the essay emphasized the potential and limitations of AI tools like ChatGPT in higher education. The essay underlined the importance of AI literacy and competency among educators, and the need for comprehensive education and training in this area. This expanded essay delves deeper into the progress made, challenges faced, and the future trajectory of AI in this sector. AI is a newer version of crude oil needing the search for its refinement and use.

AI can expand and facilitate personalized learning experiences, quickly adapting to individual learner needs and learning styles. This has significantly improved access that may, longitudinally, optimize success and innovation for an array of learner populations. Beyond academic performance, AI can help in identifying and supporting students with learning disabilities, offering customized learning paths that center individual learners' unique needs. Think of AI algorithms that analyze student performance data to tailor learning experiences that can provide targeted resources. The repetitive exercises are written to turn weaknesses into strengths. One such example, from a Stanford University study, points out that AI-driven platforms showed positive increases in student performance by up to 25%. The wider implication of AI assistance is the ability to stretch boundaries of what we originally imagined possible. The ceiling is no longer the roof for learners, and perhaps this asset, ethically used, can close the infinity loops often recognized as gaps within our systems of learning and training.

Our college has been phenomenal in our efforts to simply support the success and innovation of our entire institution. I have a great wish that since we are linked to remuneration charts and compensation studies, what about leveraging time? Yes, providing more time for the amazing people who are centered on supporting learners. As we seek to provide freedom to engage with our students even more, utilizing automation and efficiency is about creating awareness, training, and inserting application. We are early in this process and ideally, we would like to take routine tasks and streamline them through AI. This approach would afford educators even more time to focus on teaching and mentorship. Automation of activities could range from various research activities for those in the publish or perish cycles. This is where AI could be used for data analysis, predictive modeling, and assisting in the framing and solution-oriented process of research, design, and development. AI applications already range from grading of multiple-choice assessments to managing the complexities of admissions processes. The goal is to simply reduce manual workloads and improve the human connection in an age of portable devices and wearables. Moreover, Educause points out that over 60% of higher education institutions are now utilizing AI for some administrative tasks. If a survey or additional poll were issued, what would be the task(s) that we would like to automate, if we knew with certainty the responses would be ethically accurate and appropriate?

All across higher education and accreditation agencies many organizations seek to leverage data-driven insights. AI systems have provided valuable assertions into learner performance and learning outcomes which enables a more informed decision-making and curriculum design. The insights AI provides are also plausibly impactful for institutional planning, as a useful tool to predict enrollment trends and optimize resources allocation. The real time AI analytics on such important data points of student engagement, course completion rates, and learning outcomes will enable educators to adjust their teaching strategies effectively. As we learned in speech classes to adjust your speech for the audience and cadence for the listeners, we now know we also must adjust our instructional methodologies and wrap around services for the learners we serve. Institutional Research may be an area that benefits greatly from the use of AI. IBM indicates that institutions using AI for data analytics have seen a 15% improvement in retention rates. This metric is important as it casts a horizon that indicates to love the ones you are with while simultaneously indicating value for those you hope to walk alongside from micro-credential, degree, into employment.

The emergence of ethical and bias concerns regarding AI is not moot. There is still a call for critical thinking in AI integration and alignment with existing and emergent data sets is needed. The proliferation and rate of acceptance indicate more broad adoption. The continued rise of AI highlights the need for much ahead. For example, we need ethical guidelines and measures to address inherent design/algorithmic bias in AI. When we address these concerns, it must involve not just technical adjustments, but also a broader human design lens. It begs the questions, should AI tools be developed and deployed emphasizing success and innovation? Obviously, the challenge lies in ensuring AI algorithms are free from inherent bias related to such societal constructs like socioeconomic status. Moreover, MIT highlights that 35% of AI education tools do exhibit some form of bias, thus affecting their reliability and fairness. In an age where we communicate daily about the need for human connection, it is fitting that fairness, reliability, and validity serve as hot topics in the applied research domain.

A few critical questions we might consider for AI integration in Higher Education are here and need exploration:

1. How can AI be used to promote access, success, and innovation in education?

2. What are the implications of AI on academic integrity and student privacy?

3. How can we prepare educators and students for the ethical use of AI?

4. What are the long-term impacts of AI on the job market and how can education systems adapt at the appropriate need and speed of the job market and the learner?

5. What are the short-term impacts of AI on a job market that is rapidly changing to meet the adjusted needs of business and industry and the skills required?

There has been and will continue to be a need for developing comprehensive AI Literacy Programs. The journey with AI in higher education is ongoing and multifaceted. We will be required to take a balanced approach that embraces the benefits of AI while additionally addressing its challenges. Both students and educators need to be as best equipped as possible with the knowledge to use, adapt, and understand AI responsibly. In our efforts to foster ethical AI practices, institutions must lead in the development and implementation of ethical guidelines for AI use. If we choose to not advocate, AI will happen to us and not grow with us. It is important that we have agency in the narrative and the developed approaches. Moreover, collaboration between stakeholders is key. Educational institutions, policymakers, and technology experts alongside learners and industry must harness AI's full potential while mitigating its risks. A tall task in underwriting the unknown, but I think we have broad examples. Collaboration between educational institutions, technology companies, and governments is key. Such partnerships facilitate resource sharing, innovation, and responsible AI development. Additionally, global collaboration is essential for setting international standards and best practices.

The journey of integrating AI into higher education, as envisioned in the original essay, has unfolded into a multifaceted reality. It involves leveraging AI's strengths, addressing its limitations, and maintaining a focus on ethical and human-centered principles. The future of AI in higher education requires a balanced approach, combining technological advancements with ethical considerations and innovation. This comprehensive strategy is vital for harnessing AI's potential in preparing students for a rapidly evolving world and creating an education system that is both transformative and responsible. The synthesized perspectives of the theoretical and applied practical applications of AI in higher education offer a holistic view of its evolution and future trajectory. We have so much to look forward to ...

Emerging Technologies and The Evolution of Learning Part II

In the United States, advanced robotics and the Internet of Things are projected to provide an economic boost worth over $15 trillion by 2030. This digital transformation will impact workers across industries, with up to one-third of U.S. jobs potentially automated. Communities that proactively invest in retraining and reskilling will fare best in navigating this shift.

As innovations like artificial intelligence, augmented reality, and blockchain spread, they promise to fundamentally shift and reshape economies, societies around the world, and perhaps what it means to work in situ. According to recent research, over 70% of global GDP could be digitized by 2030 through smart automation, AI adoption, and Industry 4.0 technologies. Here in the southeastern region, states like Tennessee are poised to lead in next-generation technologies. With tech hubs like Nashville's "Silicon Valley of the South," our regional economy increasingly runs on innovation. Upcoming 5G and ultimately 6G infrastructure improvements across the southeast will further empower cutting – edge mobile solutions. Portability will become a norm.

Yet for all its potential, an ethical guiding hand remains vital as technology reshapes society, sustenance, sustainability. Trust in autonomous systems, fair and equal access to emergent innovations, data privacy, and broader democratization are all critical concerns. Perhaps at one point or some point, we saw ourselves and our nation as the pin head of the needle, providing balance upon many axes. We have watched as other nations have invested and sped up their abilities to become better versed technologically. As global citizens, our shared future depends on balancing rapid technological progress with conscientious implementation and regulation. Only by evolving our awareness and governance alongside our capabilities can we build an accessible and sustainable digital society where all people are empowered. The same technologies that drive Industry 4.0 hold incredible promise to lift up humanity, if deployed justly.

By preparing students and workers (learners) holistically, fostering digital literacy as well as empathy and critical analysis, educational institutions like Motlow State can help transduce coming societal shifts into positive transformations. Our role only grows in importance as graduating classes enter an increasingly automated, connected, and intelligent world. As a human, we must model the adaptable and holistic mindset we hope to impart across society. Just as educators prepare students, mentors their mentees, and officers direct their troops – we must look at technologies and contexts we work within as they evolve. Therefore, our philosophies, methodologies, and all matter of opine must evolve too.

Learning is "it" and "it" happens everywhere and all the time. In the last half century, the incorporation of innovative formats like virtual reality, flipped classrooms, and experiential learning into curricula promotes the skillsets needed to navigate an era of exponential change. Further, maintaining tight feedback loops with industry partners, policymakers, and community stakeholders helps ensure alignment between the dynamic needs of society and education. Fostering success and innovation is an interdisciplinary collaboration. This approach is vital for developing the needed well-rounded perspectives required for organizational advancement. The systemic nature of emerging technologies means no single domain holds all the answers when shaping ethical innovation. By bringing together viewpoints from technology, ethics, governance, culture and beyond, we can strive conscientious progress.

Fundamentally, the future remains a co-creation. As exponential technologies dramatically expand society's possibilities and humans provide the limits, we recognize the compound risks if handled without care. Only after evolving our collective wisdom as fast as our tools can build a world where all benefit from advancing capabilities will we recognize that tools developed must be human centered designs or bust. Moreover, the rapid pace of change can pose challenge, but challenge also represents opportunity. With ethical innovation, creative implementation and tireless compassion, educators help transcend barriers, transforming disruption into growth. Though the way forward holds uncertainties, what is certain ... is that our human capacity for resiliency, determination, and completion lights the paths. Step by step, we forge ahead.

As we forge onwards, please know that technology is merely a means, not an end. I too must be reminded intermittently in situ. Behind every innovation are our fundamental human drives – to create, to connect, to understand. By serving these core motivations consciously, we direct progress down ethical channels. At Motlow State, this people-centric philosophy guides our implementation of emerging technologies. We deploy virtual simulation not just for efficient skill building, but also to cultivate empathy by allowing students to inhabit new perspectives. We utilize AI-adaptive learning to make education more accessible, not to replace human instructors and the importance of their interactions.

Likewise, our cyber security programs teach protecting confidential data not just as a technical skill, but as an issue of respecting human dignity. And our courses embody the kind of innovation focus as much as they do mindfulness, ethics, and systemic thinking as raw computing power or quantitative efficiency. Across domains, our aim is to align digital capabilities with enduring wisdom. Technology can enhance our innate human potential for cooperation, compassion, and communication rather than distract from it. Conscientious design plus an ethos of learning further the learner as they map and extend into the digital frontier. As a point of reference, we may conclude that trial and error in any journey into uncharted spaces occurs. As educators we must grant grace – to ourselves and students – as we navigate this vast transition together. Perfection is neither possible nor the purpose; progress and persistence are the compass.

By evolving our collective skillset while staying grounded to united values, we can build a future where technology elevates rather than overwhelms humanity. With courage, care, and confidence, students can harness emerging innovations not just for personal success, but for the betterment of all global citizens. This is one of the great opportunities of our time. Looking ahead, we might consider that continuing to push the boundaries of what is possible in education is only limited by our own imagination. We must pioneer creative implementations of emerging technologies today, doing so prepares society for the potential futures whiles steering progress towards success and innovation.

Imagine immersive simulations allowing students to inhabit alternative lives, gaining firsthand exposure to initiated innovations across cultures, privileges and barriers faced by communities across the globe. Picture AI systems providing real-time feedback tailored not just to academic comprehension, but also to psychological and emotional intelligence growth. Consider augmented environments that reduce reliance on finite resources by mimicking ecologies, geographies, and extra-planetary settlements.

These visions highlight how emerging innovations applied conscientiously could profoundly transform learning, learners, and the environments from which they hail for the better. And students well-versed in flipping perspectives, interrogating biases in machine systems and recognizing planetary interconnection will become our next visionary global citizens. Obviously, to solve what is in front of us will demand that we all participate. Simultaneously, we must acknowledge current shortcomings and drifts in issues of representation, transparency and accountability that arise in applying new technologies absent proper safeguards. Progress depends on creatively overcoming these critical challenges through cross-disciplinary dialogue and again, human centered design.

By braiding cutting-edge capabilities with discernment, self-reflection and care for our shared world, we can advance both technologically and humanely. If guided by wisdom, every step brings us closer to a future liberated from barriers that obscure our common dignity. The path ahead promises both known and unknown trials and revelations. Nevertheless, the exponential growth in society's potential makes this an opportune moment. This is the moment to engage and participate in the world around us. Let us continue to innovate and dream. May we have the courage to imagine abundantly while proceeding judiciously. The vision to see and honor the past surfaces, while remaining centered and committed to elevating all the people in our ever-ascendant journey. Over the millennia's, I would have thought we would learn that we are simply better together.

ABB Robotics Education Affiliate
ABB

test
prove
robotics
robotics
robotics

Acknowledged as a strategist, connector, visionary, influencer, and implementer, Dr. Michael Torrence, a front-runner in higher education across Tennessee and the nation, is the seventh seated President of Motlow State Community College. Since arriving in May 2018, Dr. Torrence has transformed Motlow State into an award-winning, cutting-edge, innovative college year after year. He has masterfully blended the rural with the urban all the while touching students and transforming communities one at a time. His leadership and vision have placed the College on platforms and before audiences that were unknown to Motlow before his arrival.

Dr. Torrence is a technology strategist, having worked in higher education for more than 30 years. He deliberately creates space so everyone may have a voice and a seat at the table. He practices inclusive excellence and holistic development. His areas of expertise include Community and Economic Development, Research, Adult Education, Student Success, Academic Affairs, Professional Development, Distance Learning, and Success and Innovation. Additional interests are Applied Learning with Open Education Resources (OER), Virtual Reality, Augmented Reality, Mixed Reality, Automation, Robotics, Mechatronics, and Gamification as platforms for education, learning, and training business and industry to increase efficiency and scalability. Dr. Torrence is also an entrepreneurial business development professional.

Dr. Torrence serves on local, state, national, and international boards that influence and shape the future of higher education. He is the recipient of many awards crossing several categories. Recently, he was named a Distinguished Alumni by South Dakota State University, where he earned both the undergraduate and graduate degrees. He served on the American Association of Community Colleges Board and was appointed to the Community Colleges of Appalachian Board of Directors. He is a coveted Maxine Smith Fellow and is only one of two Fellows who serve as a Community College President in the Tennessee Board of Regents--the College System of Tennessee, the system that governs community and technical colleges. He is a premier speaker and lecturer. Dr. Torrence is an Air Force veteran. He earned a Ph.D. in Exceptional Learning (Literacy) from Tennessee Technological University.

www.ingramcontent.com/pod-product-compliance
Lightning Source LLC
LaVergne TN
LVHW082359200926
848481LV00012B/3614
* 9 7 9 8 3 4 8 5 5 5 6 0 3 *